The Savvy Networker

By Drs. Ron and Caryl Krannich

THE SAVVY NETWORKER

Building Your Job Net For Success

Ronald L. Krannich, Ph.D.
Caryl Rae Krannich, Ph.D.

IMPACT PUBLICATIONS
Manassas Park, VA

Library of Congress Cataloging-in-Publication Data

Krannich, Ronald L.
   The savvy networker : key skills for landing a great job / Ronald L. Krannich, Caryl Rae Krannich.
      p. cm. – (The career savvy series)
   Includes bibliographical references and index.
   ISBN 1-57023-145-1
   1. Job hunting. 2. Business networks. I. Krannich, Caryl Rae.
   II. Title. III. Series.

HF5382.K693 2001
650.14–dc21

                                       2001016576

Publisher: For information on Impact Publications, including current and forthcoming publications, authors, press kits, online bookstore, and submission requirements, visit Impact's website: *www.impactpublications.com*

Publicity/Rights: For information on publicity, author interviews, and subsidiary rights, contact the Media Relations Department: Tel. 703-361-7300, Fax 703-361-7300, or email: *network@impactpublications.com*.

Sales/Distribution: All bookstore sales are handled through Impact's trade distributor: National Book Network, 15200 NBN Way, Blue Ridge Summit, PA 17214, Tel. 1-800-462-6420. All other sales and distribution inquiries should be directed to the publisher: Sales Department, IMPACT PUBLICATIONS, 9104 Manassas Drive, Suite N, Manassas Park, VA 20111-5211, Tel. 703-361-7300, Fax 703-335-9486, or email: *sales@impactpublications.com*

Contents

CHAPTER 1

The Savvy Networker. **1**
- Childhood Behaviors You Must Change   1
- Savvy and Not-So-Savvy Networkers   2
- The Secret Language of Success   3
- What's Your "Savvy Networking I.Q."?   4
- Where Do You Go, What Do You Do?   8
- Communicate Your Qualifications to Strangers   8
- Get Amazing Results   9
- Question Success   10
- Confused, Abused, and Misused   10
- Ethical and Practical Networking   12
- Go Beyond Role Playing   13
- Change Your Behavior   15
- Coming Up   16
- The More You Explore   18

CHAPTER 2

Network For Jobs **19**
- The Four Networks   19
- Individual Level Networks   20
- Organizational Level Networks   22
- Community Level Networks   24
- Electronic Networks   28
- Networking   28

- Advertised and Hidden Job Markets   32
- Finding Jobs and Changing Careers   35
- Career Development and Job Search Processes   36
- Organize and Sequence Your Job Search   40
- Achieving Success Through Planning and Networking   41
- Do Your Homework   43

CHAPTER 3

Myths and Realities **44**
- Unfortunate Images and Myths   44
- Job Search and Work-Content Skills   45
- Finding Jobs   46
- Information, Advice, and Referrals   48
- Networking Strategies   49
- Interpersonal and Electronic Networking   51
- Resumes and Networking   53
- Resumes and Informational Interviews   54
- Informational Interviews   54
- Rejections   54
- Initiating Contacts   55
- Referrals   55
- Long-Distance Networking   56
- Cooperation   56
- Approaching Strangers   56
- Planning and Luck   57
- Additional Realities   57
- Prepare For Advice and Chaos   60

CHAPTER 4

Build Your Network **61**
- Identify Your Network   61
- Develop a Contact List   62
- Expand Your Network   64
- Build Your Networks Through Prospecting   65
- Make Many Contacts   67
- Telephone For Job Leads   69
- Minimize Rejections   71
- Be Honest and Sincere   72
- Observe the 5R's of Informational Interviewing   73

CHAPTER 5

Develop Job Leads and Conduct Interviews 74
- Employers' Needs 74
- Informational Interviews 75
- Enter the Back Door 76
- Approach the Right People 77
- Use the Telephone Frequently and Effectively 78
- Making Cold Calls For Uncovering Job Leads 84
- Calling in Response to Ads and Vacancy Announcements 86
- Effective Telephone Closings 87
- Answering Machine or Voice Mail Message 88
- Try Approach Letters and Follow-Up Calls 90
- Prepare Your Questions 97
- Conduct the Interview Well 98
- Provide Useful and Quality Information 104
- Expect Serendipity 106
- Follow Principles of Successful Networking 106

CHAPTER 6

Maintain and Expand Your Network 108
- Remember Follow-Up and Feedback 108
- Network On the Job 110
- Develop Linkages to Other Organizations 110
- Transcend the Job Search By Being In Demand 111

CHAPTER 7

Networks For Networking 113
- Professional and Trade Associations 113
- Networking Communities 114
- Information Sources 117
- Key Associations 117 ·
- The Organizations 118
- Job Search Networks 125

CHAPTER 8

Networking On the Internet. 126
- The Basics 126
- Online Networking 127
- Newsgroups and Mailing Lists 128

Index **129**

The Authors **131**

Career Resources **151**

The Savvy Networker

1

The Skilled and Effective Networker

S UCCESSFUL PROFESSIONALS TEND TO BEHAVE DIF-
ferently from others. Above all, many are savvy networkers
who know how to network their way to job and career success.
They exhibit a set of communication behaviors that can be
learned and applied to many different processes and situations.

For our purposes, finding jobs and advancing careers constitute two
of the most important processes to which networking skills can be
applied for achieving success. That's our focus—outline key networking skills for job and career success.

Childhood Behaviors You Must Change

We often become victims of our own culture and good intentions.
Indeed, most people learn two things in their childhood that may later
become detrimental to career success:

- Don't talk about other people's money—it's not your business.
- Don't talk to strangers—they may take advantage of you.

By not talking about what others make, many people later become
"salary dumb"; not knowing what they are worth, they don't do well

1

negotiating salaries and asking for raises. By avoiding contact with strangers, they often become socially and professionally inept in situations that require building relationships with important strangers.

To be successful in adulthood, many people need to change these two ingrained childhood behaviors. They especially need to learn how to talk to strangers who may become important to their career success.

Savvy and Not-So-Savvy Networkers

For some people, networking comes naturally as part of their overall orientation to others. You quickly see this in many personal and professional situations. Often being affable and extroverted individuals, savvy networkers tend to easily engage in conversations with strangers, quickly make new friends, and frequently maneuver within a large network of acquaintances for both pleasure and profit. Like salespeople, they tend to keep fat and well-worn Rolodexes filled with the names, addresses, phone numbers, and email addresses of people who are important to them—whom they can easily call upon—and who define their personal and professional networks. When attending social gatherings or professional meetings, they know how to work a room of strangers, who often get added to their bulging Rolodex. A type of social entrepreneur, savvy networkers collect and position people who populate their ever-growing network of key relationships.

> *Networking is a communication process involving the exchange of information, advice, and referrals. It's a give-and-take process with a purpose in mind.*

For more introverted individuals, networking is a difficult and unnatural experience. They would rather stay to themselves and their small network of friends than engage in the uncomfortable task of meeting strangers and engaging in awkward conversations. They tend to view their interpersonal world in terms of formal rules and regulations for greeting and meeting others. Exchanging names, addresses, and phone numbers with strangers is not something that comes naturally to them; indeed, they often appear disinterested in small talk and anxious to be somewhere else where they feel more comfortable. Unwilling to initiate conversations with strangers, they usually need formal introductions to greet and meet new people.

Whether you like it or not, networking works for those who know how to use it to their advantage—and to the possible disadvantage of others. For everyone involved, networking is a communication process involving the exchange of information, advice, and referrals. It's a give-and-take process that participants find both purposeful and rewarding.

Three Skill Sets For Success

Rather than sit passively on the sidelines waiting for jobs and promotions to come to them, savvy networkers develop proactive communication strategies that involve these three major skill sets for personal and professional success:

- making connections
- building relationships
- nurturing networks

When looking for a job, savvy networkers **make connections** for acquiring employment information and leads by using the telephone and Internet, working professional meetings and social gatherings, and writing and following up letters and email. They **build relationships** by engaging in informational interviews and following up on referrals. They **nurture or manage networks** by staying in touch and exchanging information, advice, and referrals with their "connections."

Collectively known as "networking," these activities lead to job interviews and offers. When on the job, savvy networkers view their environment as a set of strategic relationships that need to be developed and managed rather than a hierarchy of rules, regulations, authority, and perks. Using similar connecting and relationship-building and managing strategies, they empower themselves with demonstrated professional achievements that are central to accelerating their career advancement.

The Secret Language of Success

Networking, networking, networking! Everybody says they do it, but few seem to know how to do it well. They often abuse it rather than use it to their benefit.

There must be something magical in those words. For those who understand what networking is all about, this term equates with job and career success. It's the secret language of effective job seekers and career advancers. It's the key to unlocking the doors of prospective employers and scoring high on performance appraisals.

> *Networking is the key to unlocking the doors of prospective employers and scoring high on performance appraisals.*

Be it in your personal or professional life, networking can achieve amazing results. It can be applied to many different situations and settings, depending on your goals. If your goal is to find a job, networking can quickly put you in contact with employers and help you locate numerous unadvertised positions. If used properly, networking can become your ticket to job and career success. It can cut your job search time in half, put you into high quality jobs, and hasten your long-term career advancement. You will acquire the street smarts for easily changing jobs and advancing your career.

What's Your "Savvy Networking I.Q."?

Just how savvy are you when it comes to finding a job and advancing your career? Do you have the necessary networking skills for success? Can you quickly network your way to job and career success, or do you need to focus on developing specific networking skills? Let's start by testing your "Savvy Networking I.Q." You do this by responding to the following set of agree/disagree statements:

INSTRUCTIONS: Respond to each statement by circling the number to the right that best represents your situation. The higher your score, the higher your "Savvy Networking IQ."

SCALE: 5 = strongly agree   2 = disagree
             4 = agree   1 = strongly disagree
             3 = maybe, not certain

1. I enjoy going to business and social
    functions where I have an opportunity
    to meet new people. (CONNECT/
    BUILD)   5   4   3   2   1

2. I usually take the initiative in introducing myself to people I don't know. (CONNECT)   5   4   3   2   1

3. I enjoy being in groups and actively participating in group activities. (CONNECT/BUILD)   5   4   3   2   1

4. On a scale of 1 to 10, my social skills are at least a "9." (BUILD/NURTURE)   5   4   3   2   1

5. I listen carefully and give positive feedback when someone is speaking to me. (CONNECT/BUILD)   5   4   3   2   1

6. I have a friendly and engaging personality that attracts others to me. (CONNECT/BUILD/NURTURE)   5   4   3   2   1

7. I make a special effort to remember peoples' names and frequently address them by their name. (CONNECT)   5   4   3   2   1

8. I carry business cards and often give them to acquaintances from whom I also collect business cards. (CONNECT)   5   4   3   2   1

9. I have a system for organizing business cards I receive, including notes on the back of each card. (BUILD)   5   4   3   2   1

10. I seldom have a problem starting a conversation and engaging in small talk with strangers. (CONNECT)   5   4   3   2   1

11. I enjoy making cold calls and persuading strangers to meet with me. (CONNECT)   5   4   3   2   1

12. I usually return phone calls in a timely manner. (CONNECT)   5   4   3   2   1

13. If I can't get through to someone on the phone, I'll keep trying until I do, even if it means making 10 more calls. (CONNECT)   5   4   3   2   1

14. I follow up on new contacts by phone,
    email, or letter. (BUILD)   5   4   3   2   1

15. I have several friends who will give
    me job leads. (BUILD)   5   4   3   2   1

16. I frequently give and receive referrals.
    (BUILD)   5   4   3   2   1

17. I have many friends. (BUILD)   5   4   3   2   1

18. I know at least 25 people who can
    give me career advice and referrals.
    (BUILD)   5   4   3   2   1

19. I don't mind approaching people
    with my professional concerns.
    (CONNECT/BUILD)   5   4   3   2   1

20. I enjoy having others contribute to
    my success. (BUILD)   5   4   3   2   1

21. When I have a problem or face a
    challenge, I usually contact someone
    for information and advice. (BUILD)   5   4   3   2   1

22. I'm good at asking questions and
    getting useful advice from others.
    (BUILD)   5   4   3   2   1

23. I usually handle rejections in stride
    by learning from them and moving on.
    (BUILD)   5   4   3   2   1

24. I can sketch a diagram, with appropriate
    linkages, of individuals who are most
    important in both my personal and
    professional networks. (BUILD)   5   4   3   2   1

25. I regularly do online networking by
    participating in Usenet newsgroups,
    mailing lists, chats, and bulletin boards.
    (CONNECT/BUILD)   5   4   3   2   1

26. I regularly communicate my
    accomplishments to key members
    of my network. (NURTURE)   5   4   3   2   1

27. I make it a habit to stay in touch with members of my network by telephone, email, and letter. (NURTURE)   5   4   3   2   1

28. I regularly send personal notes, birthday and holiday greeting cards, and letters for special occasions to people in my network. (NURTURE)   5   4   3   2   1

29. I still stay in touch with childhood friends and old schoolmates. (NURTURE)   5   4   3   2   1

30. I have a great network of individuals who I can call on at anytime for assistance, and they will be happy to help me. (BUILD/NURTURE)   5   4   3   2   1

31. I belong to several organizations, including a professional association. (CONNECT/BUILD)   5   4   3   2   1

32. I consider myself an effective networker who never abuses his relationships. (CONNECT/BUILD/NURTURE)   5   4   3   2   1

33. Others see me as a savvy networker. (CONNECT/BUILD/NURTURE)   5   4   3   2   1

TOTAL I.Q.   _____

If your total composite I.Q. is above 155, you're most likely a savvy networker. If you're below 120, you're probably lacking key networking skills. Each of the above items indicates a particular connect, build, or nurture behavior or skill that contributes to one's overall networking effectiveness. Concentrate on improving those items on which you appear to be weak. For example, you may discover you are particularly savvy at "connecting" with people but you're weak on "building" and "nurturing" relationships—or vice versa—that define your network. Consequently, you should benefit greatly from the remainder of this book. Indeed, upon completing this book, your "Savvy Networking I.Q." should improve by at least 20 points. In the end, you'll become more proactive as you connect, build, and nurture your network for job and career success!

Where Do You Go, What Do You Do?

Success in finding employment, keeping jobs, and advancing careers involves much more than acquiring impressive educational credentials, demonstrating powerful skills and abilities, mailing outstanding resumes and letters, making cold calls, conducting an online job search, or implementing a well conceived plan of action.

Whatever your qualifications, good intentions, or Internet prowess, you must clearly communicate your qualifications and accomplishments to employers in the most efficient and effective manner possible. **You** must let potential employers know that **you** are the one who will most likely add the greatest value to their operations. **You** must motivate them to take action that favors **you**.

But how can you best communicate your qualifications to potential employers, especially given the highly competitive nature of today's job market? Let's face reality. You're competing with hundreds—perhaps thousands—of individuals who have mastered the art of responding to classified job ads with well-crafted resumes and letters or posting their resumes in electronic resume databases. Some use aggressive telephone tactics or get an inside track to employers through connections with influential people. Many even hire employment specialists to help them find a job.

Where do you go and what do you plan to do next? How are you going to chart your path to job and career success?

Communicate Your Qualifications to Strangers (Employers)

Despite all that is written and prescribed about finding jobs and changing careers, the central purpose of a job search is very simple—communicate your qualifications to potential employers. You do this by focusing on your **accomplishments** as well as providing employers with evidence of your past and present performance.

Since most employers you encounter will be strangers, you must use an approach that enables you to effectively introduce yourself to strangers and then convince these strangers that you are a high value person who should be offered a job. Needless to say, this is not your normal way of doing business with others—especially with strangers!

If you focus laser-like on this single purpose, you will be surprised how successful you will become in your job search. You'll stop wasting time on activities that contribute little or nothing to this central purpose. Again, you want to communicate your qualifications to potential employers whom you must sufficiently motivate to offer you a job.

Networking is the most important process by which you can communicate your qualifications to employers. While networking in general can enrich your social and professional life, when applied to the job search, networking becomes the key dynamic for opening the doors of employers who ordinarily would not know about you nor seriously consider you for a job. It is this process—networking —that you can and must learn and put into practice if you are to become most effective in your job search as well as once you are on the job.

> *The central purpose of a job search is very simple – communicate your qualifications to potential employers. You can do this effectively by networking.*

Get Amazing Results

That's our task in the following pages—to show you how networking skills play a central role in conducting an effective job search as well as in getting ahead in your career. Page after page provide you with practical advice on how to develop your own networking skills which you can immediately put into practice with amazing results.

If you follow our guidance, you should more than double your job search effectiveness. You will learn to communicate your qualifications loudly and clearly to hundreds of potential employers you would have failed to contact had you not discovered this book. Better still, once you get the job, you will continue to use your networking skills to ensure your future job and career success.

While your job future may appear uncertain, with sound networking skills you need never be without a job. Chances are you will find jobs and advance in careers that are a "fit" for your particular mix of motivated interests, skills, and abilities.

Question Success

Why are some people more successful at finding jobs and advancing careers than others? Are they more intelligent, skilled, and motivated than the average person? Perhaps they are luckier or they have the right connections to people who have the power to hire.

Or perhaps they do something different from others when looking for employment or advancing on the job.

Maybe they are well organized and have a clear idea of what they want to do. They probably write excellent resumes and letters, target key individuals and organizations, and perform well in job interviews. Could they also be excellent networkers?

How can you best find a job and advance your career in today's job market? Is it proper to influence the hiring process by using "connections" to bypass formal hiring procedures? When and how should one use others in gaining access to employers as well as getting ahead on the job?

What is this thing called "networking" that everyone talks about when looking for jobs? Is it something you need to learn and use in your own job search?

These questions frequently confront individuals who are conducting a job search or attempting to advance their career within an organization. They are central concerns in the pages that follow. For these questions need to be addressed in practical how-to terms so you will have a better understanding of how to identify, build, and use your own networks for finding jobs and advancing your career in the years ahead.

Confused, Abused, and Misused

Few terms are so confused, abused, and misused as "networks" and "networking." The confusion, misuse, and abuse take place on both the conceptual and practical levels. It's a WYKWIM—*"Well, You Know What I Mean"*—concept. Indeed, the concepts are seldom clearly defined. Job seekers and career advancers, for example, are told they should use their "networks" to get ahead, and the key to job search success is "networking." Therefore, some of the so-called facts of job search life are that *"You have to network"* and *"Networking is the key to uncovering job leads, getting job interviews, and being promoted on the job."* The terms are used so freely that one assumes everyone should know what this is all about and that many are doing it with considerable success!

On a more practical level, job seekers are often told that networking involves *"contacting the people who have the power to hire,"* as if busy hiring officials have nothing better to do than to be pestered by job seekers who ostensibly only want "information and advice" rather than a "job interview and offer." Or they are told to join professional associations that will provide them with networking opportunities—as if other members of the organization have nothing better to do than to be bothered by "networkers" who have little interest in an organization other than using it to exchange business cards and collect names, addresses, telephone numbers, and email addresses for uncovering job leads which, in turn, lead to pestering even more people in one's new-found network. Indeed, we know some people, including ourselves, who have dropped their membership in professional associations precisely because they have become popular centers for "networkers" who abuse the organization for their own employment gains. They be come dens of textbook networkers—name-droppers and business card exchangers who want nothing more than to collect more names and referrals for building and using their own networks.

> *Many career counselors are reluctant to recommend networking strategies because of so many networking abuses by aggressive job seekers.*

The basic problem with networks and networking lies with those who recommend the building and use of networks and networking. On the one hand, writers tell you networks and networking are important, but they never define these terms in practical how-to terms. At best they outline "principles" of networking, present vague examples of what networking involves, or include anecdotal cases of successful networking.

On the other hand, many writers give practical guidance that often leads to the very abuses that give networking such a bad name—contact those who have the power to hire and join professional associations. They legitimize an aggressive job seeker who attempts to acquire influence in the hiring process. As a result, many career counselors are reluctant to recommend networking strategies, or they rightfully criticize it as being overstated and overrated in importance as well as frequently abusive in application.

Ethical and Practical Networking

We believe networking is the key process for conducting a successful job search as well as for keeping jobs and advancing careers. However, networks and networking need to be better defined and specified in both ethical and practical how-to terms than heretofore attempted. The confusion, abuses, and misuses of networks and networking must be avoided if you are to develop and use networks to their maximum advantage. Our approach does not require you to become an extroverted, aggressive salesperson who uncovers new job leads through cold-calling methods. Nor do you need to deceive others or abuse organizations by playing an "information and advice" game when you are actually attempting to use people to get "job interviews and offers."

Role players eventually will be discovered for what they really are – deceptive job applicants who behave very differently on the job.

Our approach to networks and networking begins with a basic ethical emphasis:

You must be completely honest with both yourself and others when seeking employment or advancing your career.

While you can learn to play new roles for new situations, such role playing involves acting out scripts that are unfamiliar to most people. These role players eventually will be discovered for what they really are—individuals who may behave very differently on the job from the role they learned to temporarily play in order to get a job interview and offer. Once they get the job and begin displaying their normal patterns of behavior—that have little relationship to the roles they played in getting the job—they may experience on-the-job difficulties that will require something more than an additional round of newly acquired role-playing behaviors. Their employer may discover he has once again been deceived by a candidate who learned all the "ins" and "outs" of getting a job interview and offer—another good networker who knew how to get the job interview and offer but a poor job performer.

Our approach to networks and networking is also practical. We go beyond examples of successful networking and listings of networking sources to provide you with the basic building blocks for identifying, developing, and using your own networks in the process of finding employment and advancing your career. Our concepts are defined so they can be translated into practical use. In so doing, we include models and examples designed to build key networking skills. Once you translate these concepts into practical use by following the models and examples, you should be able to make networking a permanent part of your job and career behavior. Above all, you need not develop a new personality nor become an aggressive and manipulative individual intent on making others do things your way.

Go Beyond Role Playing

Most job search advice is based on a very simple principle that makes the job search both easy and difficult for most people: learn to play different roles for different situations. For some people, role playing is easy; they learn the expectations of others, copy examples, and change their behavior accordingly. Consequently, if employers want to see candidates who are energetic, competent, and likable, then you should dish out energy, competence, and likability on resumes and in interviews by the way you write (use action verbs, keywords, and focus on achievements), talk (use positives and be enthusiastic), and appear in person (dress for success).

While this role approach makes sense, because it is designed to meet employers' expectations—and at times exceed them—this approach is very difficult for many individuals to follow because it requires role playing which does not come naturally to them. Outside the make-believe world of the theater and movies, playing a role in real life—especially when looking for a job—verges on being dishonest with others: you must temporarily behave like someone you are not in order to get and pass the job interview. To be told to acquire a temporary set of new behaviors—to take on stage before strangers who have the power to hire—is beyond both the motivation and capacity of most individuals. Making cold calls to uncover job leads or contacting people with the power to hire may make sense in a job search, but these activities are best done by people who are naturally assertive, aggressive, and perhaps obnoxious in their relations with strangers. They simply don't come naturally to many people who are choosy about how and with whom they associate.

Such role playing also borders on being unethical sales tactics. Emphasizing form over substance, such role playing does not reveal the individual's real qualifications nor project future performance in meaningful ways. Worst of all, this approach results in canned and meaningless resume language (*"Enjoy working with people"*) and stock answers to interview questions (*"My education helped prepare me..."*) that raise troubling questions about what information is actually being exchanged in the job search and hiring processes. Are you communicating your qualifications or manipulating forms in lieu of content? It's not surprising that role playing often confuses form with content.

For employers, this process at times becomes a disappointing role-playing ritual of sorts. After interviewing the 100th candidate dressed in a similar blue suit, carrying a leather briefcase, communicating positive nonverbal behaviors (firm handshake and good eye contact), and answering all the questions according to the textbook, employers begin wondering about the efficacy of engaging themselves and candidates in the traditional recruitment and evaluation processes. These processes may have for all intents and purposes been negated by well prepared candidates who know how to play the proper roles of "good applicant" and "good interviewee." They are well-versed in key job search "strategies and techniques" that are supposed to really work for getting a job. No wonder interviewers increasingly opt for conducting behavior-based interviews that cut through most of the traditional interview role playing, or require some form of testing (skill, psychological, attitudinal) as they attempt to get at predicting the real performance capabilities of candidates.

Contrary to what many job search strategies and techniques may suggest, employers are not stupid. They still look for content, substance, and value—the key elements that define the value of jobs. They want to accurately predict performance rather than risk hiring a potential problem employee.

A more ethical and realistic approach to the job search and career advancement is one that focuses on building new skills rather than a new set of role behaviors. Therefore, we are concerned with the process of building and using networks as a permanent aspect of your career rather than something you only do when you need to find a job or advance your career. The skill becomes part of your daily patterns of behavior. As such, it becomes natural and reveals the real you.

Change Your Behavior

Each of us has learned behaviors, habits, or patterns we reinforce daily. Many of these behaviors generate positive responses from others; but some are bad habits we should break. For example, how well do you communicate over the telephone or Internet, physically appear to others, or ask and answer questions? Do you mumble, fidget, or lose eye contact when nervous? Do you talk too much or too little? Are you too shy to contact strangers? Do you have a habit of being late for appointments? These are examples of behaviors we can change if strongly **motivated** to do so. But it is easy to slip back into the old patterns if we are not careful.

If you feel you need to break certain habits and learn new behaviors, you can make long-term changes without resorting to temporary role playing. You must first be aware of the undesirable behavior you wish to replace as well as the desirable behavior you wish to acquire. Second, you must be aware of the undesirable behavior whenever it takes place. For this you may need to enlist the aid of your spouse or good friend; ask them to: *"Please observe me and inform me whenever I am doing ____ _____."* After a while you will develop greater awareness of the particular behavior.

> *Contrary to what many job search techniques may suggest, employers are not stupid. They still look for content, substance, and value.*

Once we are conscious of our behavior, gradually we will become alert to our behavior early enough to alter it. Given even more time of diligent awareness, the new behavior replaces the old one and eventually becomes as natural as the undesirable behavior once was. By incorporating the new behavior into your ongoing patterns of behavior, you will learn to go beyond role playing that pervades much of the well-meaning advice on how to conduct an effective job search.

Developing an effective networking campaign that leads to getting a job that is right for you should be sufficient reason to motivate you to change some of your behaviors. If you think a behavior may be holding you back, try changing it now. The more time you give yourself, the more likely the change will become permanent and the less likely you will slip back into your former behavior.

Coming Up

This is not a book primarily about where the networks are and how you can use them to get a job or advance your career. Nor is this a book about networking in general or electronic networking via the Internet. As we will see in Chapters 7 and 8 (pages 113-128), there are numerous online and offline resources for identifying organizations that function as networks. These organizations can play an important role in finding, keeping, and advancing jobs and careers. Other books examine useful networking techniques such as small talk and mingling in groups for business and social purposes. And still others focus solely on electronic networking or interpersonal networking. This book, instead, focuses on networks and networking for the purpose of finding jobs and advancing careers both interpersonally and electronically. It shows you how to identify, expand, engage, use, develop, and maintain networks appropriate to your own job and career goals. As such, this book focuses on **developing both interpersonal and electronic networking skills** that can be used in many different settings and situations.

The chapters that follow are designed to be "user-friendly." They proceed from a definition of key concepts to explanations of how to identify, develop, and use networks as part of your permanent skill pattern for finding jobs and advancing your career. Chapter 2, *"Network For Jobs,"* outlines the major concepts central to the remaining chapters. Here we define the concepts of networks and networking and show how they relate to job search techniques, processes, and goals. The chapter assists you in identifying your own network as well as illustrates how your network can be linked to the networks of others. In this chapter we also identify seven steps in the job search process that are central to understanding the key role networking plays in the job search. The chapter concludes with a discussion of how networking relates to your overall job search campaign.

Chapter 3, *"Myths and Realities,"* examines 19 key myths and several additional realities surrounding the use and abuse of networks and networking. These myths and realities are responsible for many networking and job search failures. Moreover, they discourage many individuals from developing what we see as positive networking skills that are both ethical and practical. By outlining the realities of these myths, we attempt to put to rest the objections to networking by those who criticize it for all the wrong reasons—its misuses and abuses—and clarify many of the issues surrounding networks and networking in the job search.

Chapter 4, *"Build Your Network,"* begins looking at the practical steps in the networking process by first examining your present network of relationships and then suggesting techniques—prospecting and networking—for expanding your networks. It concludes with a discussion of how to handle one of the most important problems encountered in the process of building networks—potential rejections.

Chapter 5, *"Develop Job Leads and Conduct Interviews,"* takes you face-to-face with network contacts and potential employers by examining the major use of networks in the job search process—the informational interview. Beginning with the perspective of employers, we then turn to the job seeker in focusing on the details of approaching people by telephone and letter as well as meeting them in person for the purpose of acquiring information, advice, and referrals. This chapter includes examples of effective letters and conversations. By way of summary it outlines key rules for networking success.

Chapter 6, *"Maintain and Expand Your Network,"* stresses the importance of networking as an ongoing process for advancing one's career within an organization or profession. Stressing that networking is more than just another job-finding technique, to be most effective, it must include follow-up, feedback, and routine networking activities within and between organizations.

Chapter 7, *"Networks For Networking,"* switches from the interpersonal process of networking to examples of formal professional organizations that function as important sources for building and maintaining your networks and networking activities. These organizations serve as starting points from which you can continue developing your own long-term networking skills.

Chapter 8, *"Networking On the Internet,"* identifies several websites that constitute new arenas for job networking, from commercial employment sites to Usenet newsgroups and mailing lists.

The More You Explore

Networking is not something you can turn on and off. As both a skill and an ongoing process, networking is something individuals can and do learn. Some people are excellent networkers who acquired the skill as part of their early childhood development. They easily make friends and acquaintances and surround themselves with many individuals who can assist them in different ways. Making the right moves, they easily advance their careers by attending to the right schools, joining the right organizations, and knowing the right people who like and trust them. They are simply good at developing, using, and nurturing personal relationships to their benefit.

However, most people are less extroverted and concerned with developing and maintaining personal relationships than the example of the savvy networker. They must work at identifying, connecting, building, nurturing, and using it for job and career success. If pointed in the right direction with a few basic networking skills, these individuals also can achieve greater job and career success.

This book is all about developing basic networking skills that will enable you to further build and expand your networks in the coming years. It's a skill you can learn and use to ensure future job and career success. If you are like many other individuals who have learned our principles and put them into practice, you'll achieve amazing results as you put these networking skills to use. If you follow our advice and put a few of our tips into practice, you should be able to add an important networking component to your job and career success!

2

Network For Jobs

WHAT EXACTLY ARE NETWORKS AND THE PRO-
cess of networking, and how do they relate to you and
your job search? These questions are central to any discussion of finding jobs and advancing careers. Answers
to these questions provide the basic foundation from which you can
develop your own successful networking activities which, in turn,
should lead to a successful job search.

The Four Networks

Not surprisingly, there are as many different definitions of networks as
there are examples of networks. Most examinations of networking only
focus on one network level—the individual—in an attempt to demonstrate how the individual can improve his or her personal competency
or power in a variety of situations. However, there are other network
levels which need to be related to the individual. For our purposes, we
define and illustrate networks at four important levels in the job search
process:

- individual
- organization
- community
- electronic

19

If you want to be successful in your job search, you must be aware of all four levels of networks as well as know how each level is linked, or relates, to the other. Distinctions among these levels are necessary simply because most individuals simultaneously function at all four levels. You are, for example, an individual when you deal with other individuals. However, you also deal with organizations, and individuals and organizations are the building blocks of communities which, in turn, make up societies. You may also participate in an Internet-based electronic network or community—variously defined as newsgroups, mailing lists, chat groups, community forums, and message boards—which may provide useful information and contacts relevant to finding a job.

> *Electronic networks may play a key role in conducting an effective long-distance job search.*

If you wish to move from one community to another—conduct a "long-distance" job search—you should be aware that the networks of individuals must be linked to networks of organizations that define opportunities in communities. Electronic networks may play a key role in conducting an effective long-distance job search. These distinctions and linkages will become clearer as we further define networks through several illustrations and examples.

Individual Level Networks

At the **individual level**, your network is your interpersonal environment. It consists of individuals you know, who are important to you, and with whom you interact at different times and occasions. Many of the people you interact with most frequently have a major influence on your behavior. Other individuals may also influence your behavior, but you interact with them less frequently. While you may know and interact with hundreds of people, on a day-to-day basis you probably encounter no more than 20 people.

The figure on page 21 outlines a hypothetical network which we will again refer to in Chapter 4 when we begin identifying your own network. For now, this network consists of people with whom you have frequent contact in face-to-face situations. Within your network, some people are more important to you than others. You like some more than

Your Network of Relationships

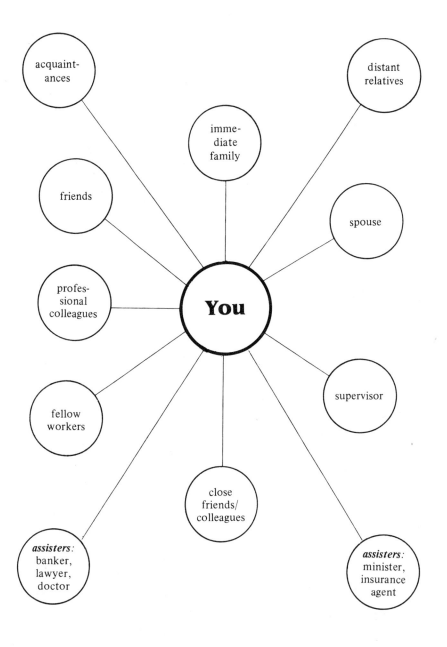

others. And some will be more helpful to you in your job search and advancement than others. Your basic network will most likely encompass the following individuals and groups: friends, acquaintances, immediate family, distant relatives, professional colleagues, spouse, supervisor, fellow workers, close friends, mentor, and local business people and professionals, such as your banker, lawyer, doctor, minister, and insurance agent. These individuals will play a central role in your networking activities as you activate your network for the purpose of acquiring information, advice, and referrals relevant to your job search and long-term career goals.

Organizational Level Networks

At the **organizational level**, networks consist of interacting positions, groups, offices, departments, and other organizational subdivisions and units that define both the formal and informal structure of an organization. Examples of typical elements defining an organization's network are supervisor, personnel office, planning unit, training office, and committees. As illustrated on page 23, these elements interact in defining the unique structure of most organizations. They also link one organization to another. They are a few of many contact points toward which individuals target their organizational networking activities. Organizational networks also include important **professional associations** that function both inside and outside organizations. As again illustrated in the figure on page 23, personnel officers or training personnel from thousands of different organizations, for example, may be members of one or two national personnel associations that publish newsletters and journals; host a community website complete with chat groups and online employment services; sponsor local chapter meetings and annual conferences; and operate job placement activities. Many members use their associations as forums for making professional contacts, building networks, and changing jobs and careers when necessary. Such organizations become key arenas for making connections, building

> *Professional organizations are key arenas for making connections, building relationships, and nurturing networks across organizational lines.*

Organizational Networks

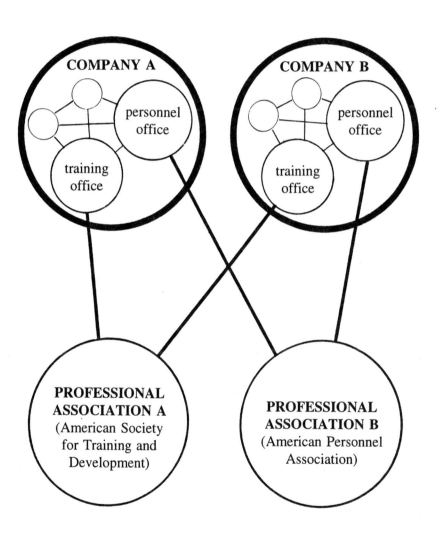

relationships, and nurturing networks across organizational lines. It's this organizational setting and its networking resources that play such important roles in the career development of its individual members.

The role of professional associations in linking personnel from one organization to another challenge popular notions of loyalty to a single organization. Professional associations tend to emphasize professional competence and loyalty to one's profession. In such an organizational situation, job and career advancement takes place through the process of networking for jobs in different organizations which have similar professional positions. Loyalty to one's professional association often takes precedence over commitment to one's current job in any one particular organization.

At the organizational level, an individual's network therefore consists of much more than those individuals they interact with on a daily basis. Their organizational level of networks consists of **opportunity structures**, such as professional associations, that enable them to link and expand their networks into other organizations with relative ease.

Community Level Networks

At the **community level**, networks consist of different organizations that define the structure of communities and enable individuals to gain access to new job and career opportunities through the combined processes of individual, organizational, and community networking. Each community, for example, has its own social, economic, political, and job market structure. The degree of structure differs for every community. However, one thing is relatively predictable: **most communities lack a coherent structure for processing job information efficiently and effectively**. Identifying these organizations and knowing how they interact with each other is key to making a **long-distance job search** in an unfamiliar community where standard networking strategies designed primarily at the individual level may or may not function well in reference to the local power structure.

Let's illustrate this level of networks with a few examples. Each community is made up of numerous individuals, groups, organizations, and institutions that are involved in pursuing their own interests in both cooperation and competition with one another. The Yellow Pages of your telephone book best outline the major actors. Banks, mortgage companies, advertising firms, car dealers, schools, churches, small businesses, industries, hospitals, law firms, governments, and civic and voluntary groups do their "own thing" and have their own internal power structure. No one dominates except in small communities which also may be company towns—mills, mining companies, publishing firms, universities, aerospace, and the military. At the same time, the groups overlap with each other because of economic, political, social, and professional needs. The banks, for example, need to loan money to the businesses and churches. The businesses, in turn, need the educational institutions. And the educational institutions need the businesses to absorb their graduates. Therefore, individuals tend to cooperate to ensure that people playing the other games also succeed. Members of school boards, medical boards, and the boardrooms of banks and corporations will overlap and give the appearance of a "power structure" even though power is structured in the loosest sense of the term. The players

Each community has its own set of "opportunity structures" for targeting your job search. These structures overlap, compete, cooperate, and co-op each other – perfect targets for your networking.

in this game compete and cooperate with each other as well as co-op one another. The structures they create can become **your opportunity structures for penetrating the hidden job market.**

Take the example of Washington, DC. The opportunity structures for your job search networks at all three levels—community, organizational, and individual—are relatively well defined in this city. While government is the major institution, other institutions are also well defined in relation to the government, especially the bulging high-tech and information technology industries. Within government, both the political and administrative institutions function as alternative opportunity structures in the Washington networks: congressional staffs, congressional committees, congressional subcommittees, congressional bureaucracy, executive staff, departments, independent executive agencies, and independent regulatory agencies. Outside, but clinging to, government are a variety of other groups and networks: interest groups, the media, professional associations, contractors, consultants, law firms, banks, and universities and colleges. As illustrated on page 26, these groups are linked to one another for survival and advancement. Charles

Community Level Networks As Opportunity Structures For Washington, DC

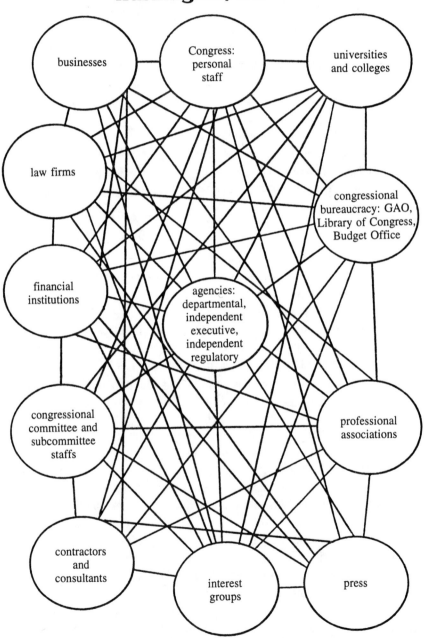

Peters (*How Washington Really Works*) calls them "survival networks" which function in the "make believe world" of Washington, DC. Ripley and Franklin (*Congress, Bureaucracy, and Public Policy*) identify the key political dynamics as "subgovernments"—the interaction of interest groups, agencies, and congressional committees. For the purposes of finding jobs and advancing careers, we call these your "**opportunity structures**" for getting ahead in the community regardless of its location.

For many years Washington insiders have learned how to use these "opportunity structures" to advance their careers. They illustrate how networks at the individual, organizational, and community level are used simultaneously for getting jobs and advancing careers. A frequent career pattern might be to work in an agency for three to four years. During that time, one would make important contacts on Capitol Hill with congressional staffs and committees as well as with private consultants, contractors, and interest groups. One's specialized knowledge on the inner workings of government is marketable to these other people. Therefore, it is relatively easy to make a job change from a federal agency to a congressional committee or to an interest group. After a few years here, you move to another group in the network. Perhaps you work on your law degree at the same time so that in another five years you can go into the one truly growth industry in the city—law firms. The keys to making these moves are the personal contacts—whom you know—and networking. Particular attention is given to keeping a current OF-612, SF 171, or resume (acceptable federal government application forms), just in case an opportunity happens to come your way. Congressional staff members usually last no more than two years; they set their sights on consulting and contracting firms, agencies, or interest groups for their next job move.

Whatever community you decide to focus your job search on, expect it to have its particular networks. Indeed, while you should view your relations with other people as a set of networks that define your interpersonal environment, you also should view communities in similar terms—they consist of networks of organizations, groups, and individuals. Do as much research as possible to identify the structure of the networks as well as the key people who can provide access to various elements that define community opportunity structures. Washington is not unique in this respect; it is just better known, and Washingtonians talk about it more because of their frequent job moves and their constant use of networking strategies for finding employment.

Electronic Networks

Electronic networks help integrate individual, organizational, and community networks. A recent and rapidly evolving innovation in the employment business, electronic networks include several computerized membership-based groups—also known as computerized job or resume banks—which are designed to quickly link candidates to employers through the use of search-and-retrieval computer software. Joining one of these networks enables users to gain access to hundreds of nationwide employers. But the majority of electronic job search options include a variety of online employment services on the Internet, such as Monster.com, CareerBuilder.com, Headhunter.net, NationJob.com, HotJobs.com, Career Web.com, CareerCity.com, BestJobs USA.com, and JobTrak.com. Free to job seekers, most of these services include thousands of job listings, searchable resume databases, job search tips, chat groups, community forums, and bulletin boards that enable users to identify job vacancies, post resumes, acquire career counseling, and network for information, advice, and referrals. Chapter 8 outlines these and other electronic networks that add a new dimension to traditional job search and networking strategies.

Most electronic job services include thousands of job listings, searchable resume databases, community forums, bulletin boards, and chat groups – great places for networking.

Networking

Networking is both a technique and a process centered around specific goals. As a technique, networking involves purposefully developing relations with others. Networking as a job search technique involves connecting and interacting with other individuals by means of prospecting, networking, and informational interviewing. Its purpose is to exchange information and acquire advice and referrals that will assist you in promoting your ultimate job search goal—getting job interviews and offers. Through the process of networking you build, expand, and activate your networks:

Techniques, Processes, and Goals of Networking

Techniques	Processes	Goals
Prospecting	Identifying and building networks	Develop a networking strategy
Networking	Linking and expanding networks	Establish contacts that lead to informational interviews
Informational interviews	Networking to achieve goals	Acquire key information, advice, and referrals that will lead to job interviews and offers

The process of networking involves both identifying your own networks (page 21) as well as linking your networks to the networks of others. As illustrated on page 30, you expand your network by linking it to the networks of other individuals who also have job information and contacts. Through the process of networking, you ask people in your basic network for referrals to individuals in their networks. This approach will greatly enlarge your basic job search network.

Examples of networking abound within the job search. You are interested in learning about job opportunities with XYZ Company, but you don't know anyone who works there. You ask a friend if she knows anyone who works for XYZ Company. She, in turn, refers you to John Taylor who retired from XYZ company two years ago. You call John Taylor and mention that your friend suggested that you give him a call because he was someone who might be able to provide you with information on XYZ Company. You meet with John Taylor and learn a great deal about the internal operations of the company. In addition, John Taylor provides you with the names of three individuals who presently work at XYZ Company and who would be willing to talk to you about your career interests. You contact these individuals, conduct informational interviews with them, and begin gaining access to the

Linking Your Networks to Others

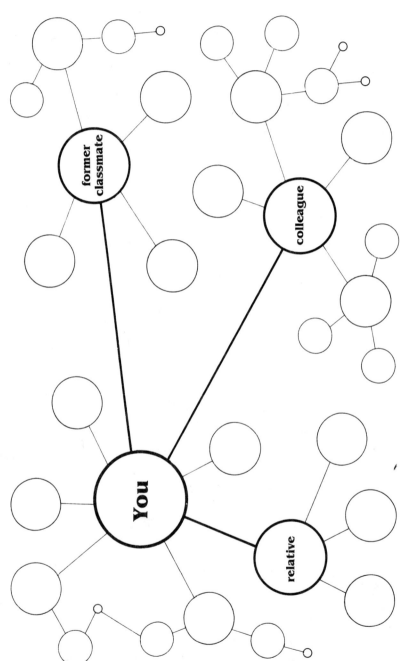

hidden job market within the company. This process continues as you receive additional referrals to individuals within the company who know about job vacancies and who make hiring decisions.

Take another example to illustrate how this might work in the case of a **long-distance job search**. You may live in Indianapolis, Indiana and wish to relocate to Orlando, Florida. While you know a great deal about Florida and living in Orlando (cost of living, housing, community activities, recreational opportunities, Disney World), you know little about job and career opportunities there. In need of conducting a long-distance job campaign, you wonder how you can find a job in Orlando while living in Indianapolis. You should first go to the Internet to check on community websites which provide a wealth of useful information on Orlando, from local news to restaurants, shops, arts, sports, and housing: *www.orlando.com, www.orlando.citysearch.com,* and *www. home.digitalcity.com/orlando.* Most such sites include information on employment, including job listings. Next, you may want to subscribe to or access online the Orlando newspaper (*www.orlandosentinel.com*) to survey the "Help Wanted" section of the classifieds (*www.orlando sentinel.com/jobs*) and respond to job vacancy announcements that seem appropriate to your skills, interests, and experience. However, if you receive no encouraging replies, you may decide it's time to begin conducting a long-distance networking campaign. You begin doing this by contacting your university alumni association at Ohio State University for names of alumni who now live in the Orlando area and who would be willing to talk to you about your job and career interests. They provide you with a list of six graduates whom you contact by letter and telephone. They indicate they will be happy to assist you with information, advice, and referrals. Since these individuals have moved into prominent positions within the community, their information, advice, and referrals appear to be invaluable to your job search. After contacting these individuals and their referrals by letter and telephone, you decide it is now time to visit Orlando for 10 days to further expand your newly developed Orlando network. During your 10-day visit, you further expand your network by meeting with 33 individuals who provide you with more information, advice, and referrals. During this time you also conduct two job interviews based on newly acquired referrals. One interview results in a job offer, which you accept. You now return to Indianapolis to make arrangements for moving to Orlando within the next two months. You are evidence that long-distance networking was the key to landing this job.

Advertised and Hidden Job Markets

Networks and networking play a central role in finding jobs and changing careers because of the particular structure of the job market. The so-called "job market" actually consists of two structurally different arenas for locating job opportunities—one advertised and another hidden. Both are characterized by a high degree of decentralization, fragmentation, and chaos. Neither should be underestimated nor overestimated when conducting a job search.

The **advertised job market** consists of job vacancy announcements and listings found on websites and in newspapers, professional and trade journals, and newsletters as well as through employment agencies and personnel offices. With more and more employers using the Internet for recruiting, make sure your job search includes an Internet component, from entering your resume into online resume databases to surveying online job vacancies. But don't expect instant results. Many job seekers find the Internet to be a waste of time—seductive but ineffective. It represents a passive job search approach. Networking, on the other hand, is a proactive approach that puts you in direct contact with real employers.

Make sure your job search includes an Internet component, from entering your resume into online resume databases to surveying online job vacancies.

Most people focus on this advertised job market because it is relatively easy to find, it looks organized, and they believe it accurately reflects available job vacancies at any given moment. In reality, however, the advertised job market probably represents no more than 40 percent of actual job openings. Furthermore, this market tends to represent positions at the extreme ends of the job spectrum—low-paying unskilled or high-paying highly skilled jobs, i.e., jobs that are hard to fill by other, less expensive, means. The majority of positions lying between these two extremes are not well represented in the listings. Competition often is great for the low- and middle-level positions. Worst of all, many of these advertised jobs are either nonexistent or were filled prior to the appearance of the ad.

You should spend a minimum amount of time—no more than 30

percent—looking for employment in the advertised job markets. Monitor this market, but don't assume it represents the entire spectrum of job opportunities. Your job search time and money are better spent elsewhere—on the hidden job market. When you identify an advertised position that is right for you, email, fax, or mail a cover letter and resume and follow up with a telephone call—but keep moving on to other potential opportunities.

However, you will find exceptions to this general rule of avoiding the advertised job market, especially in reference to new developments on the Internet. Each occupational specialty has its own internal recruitment and job finding structure. Some occupations are represented more by professional listing and recruitment services than others. Indeed, as we increasingly become a high-tech society, greater efforts will be made by both government and the private sector to increase the efficiency of employment communication by centralizing listings and recruitment services for particular occupational specialties. These services will be designed to reduce the **lag time** between when a job becomes vacant and is filled. Computerized job banks and online career centers with recruitment and employment databases, such as America's Job Bank (*www.ajb.org*), Monster.com (*www.monster.com*), and CareerBuilder. com (*www.careerbuilder.com*), will increasingly be used by employers to locate qualified candidates, and vice versa. Employers in a high-tech society need to reduce lag time as much as possible given the increasing interdependency of positions in high-tech industries. If and when such employment services and job banks become available for your occupational specialty, you should at least investigate them. In the meantime, since the job market will remain relatively disorganized in the foreseeable future, do your research and use job search strategies, such as networking, which are appropriate for this type of job market.

Your research should center on one of the key dynamics to finding employment—helping employers solve their hiring problems. Many employers turn to the advertised job market **after** they fail to recruit candidates by other, less formal and public, means. The lag time between when a position becomes vacant, is listed, and then filled is a critical period for your attention and **intervention with networking strategies**. Your goal should be to locate high quality job vacancies before they are listed.

The **hidden job market** is where the action is. It is this job market that should occupy most of your attention. Although this job market lacks a formal structure, 60 percent or more of all job opportunities are found here. Your task is to give this market some semblance of structure and coherence so that you can effectively penetrate it. If you can do this, the hidden job market will yield numerous job interviews and offers that should be right for you.

Networking is the key to penetrating the hidden job market. Consider, for example, the hiring problems of employers by putting yourself in their place. Suppose one of your employees suddenly gives you a two-week notice, or you terminate someone. Now you have a problem; you must hire a new employee. It takes time and it is a risky business you would prefer to avoid. After hours of reading resumes and interviewing, you still will be hiring an unknown who might create new problems for you.

Networking is the key to penetrating the hidden job market. It will help minimize your time and risks.

Like many other employers, you want to **minimize your time and risks**. You can do this by networking with your friends and acquaintances —contacting them to let them know you are looking for someone; you would appreciate it if they could **refer** some good candidates to you. Based on these contacts, you should receive referrals. At the same time, you want to hedge your bets, as well as fulfill affirmative action and equal opportunity requirements, by listing the job vacancy in the newspaper, with your personnel office, or through an online employment service. While 300 people respond by mail to your classified ad, you also get referrals from the trusted individuals in your network. In the end, you conduct 10 telephone interviews and three face-to-face interviews. You hire the **best** candidate—the one your former classmate recommended to you on the first day you informed her of your need to fill the vacancy. You are satisfied with your excellent choice of candidates; you are relatively certain this new employee will be a good addition to your organization.

This scenario is played out regularly in many organizations. In fact, some companies institutionalize this networking process by offering employees "finder fees" for referring qualified candidates to the company. It demonstrates the importance of getting into the interpersonal networks of the hidden job market and devoting most of your time and energy there. If you let people know you are looking for employment, chances are they will keep you in mind and refer you to others who may have an unexpected vacancy. Your networking activities will help you enter and maneuver within this job market of interpersonal networks and highly personalized information exchanges.

Finding Jobs and Changing Careers

If you are looking for your first job, reentering the job market after a lengthy absence, or planning a job or career change, you will join an army of millions of individuals who do so each year. Indeed, more than 15 million people find themselves unemployed each year. Millions of others try to increase their satisfaction within the workplace as well as advance their careers by looking for alternative jobs and careers. If you are like most other Americans, you will make more than 10 job changes and between three and five career changes during your lifetime.

Most people make job or career transitions by accident. They do little other than take advantage of opportunities that may arise unexpectedly. While chance and luck do play important roles in finding employment, we recommend that you plan for future job and career changes so that you will experience even greater degrees of chance and luck!

Finding a job or changing a career in a systematic and well-planned manner is hard yet rewarding work. The task should first be based upon a clear understanding of the key ingredients that define jobs and careers. Starting with this understanding, you should next convert key concepts into action steps for implementing your job search.

A career is a series of related jobs which have common skill, interest, and motivational bases. You may change jobs several times without changing careers. But once you change skills, interests, and motivations, you change careers.

It's not easy to find a job given the present structure of the job market. You will find the job market to be relatively disorganized, although it projects an outward appearance of coherence. If you seek comprehensive, accurate, and timely job information, the job market will frustrate you with its poor communication. While you will find many employment services ready to assist you, such services tend to be fragmented and their performance is often disappointing. Job search methods are controversial and many are ineffective, including many online career services.

No system is organized to give people jobs. At best you will encounter a decentralized and fragmented system consisting of job listings in newspapers, trade journals, and employment offices or on the Internet —all designed to link potential candidates with available job openings. Many people will try to sell you job information as well as questionable job search services. While efforts continue to create a nationwide computerized job bank (America's Job Bank, *www.ajb.org*) that would list available job vacancies on a daily basis, don't expect such initiatives to be complete nor useful for your particular employment situation.

> *Your best friend will be you. Organize a coherent job search campaign centered around networking strategies for penetrating the hidden job market.*

Many of the listed jobs may be non-existent, at a low skill and salary level, or represent only a few employers. In the end, most of the systems organized to help you find a job do not provide you with the information you need in order to land a job that is most related to your skills and interests. When looking for employment, your best friend will be you. Hopefully you will have organized a coherent job search campaign centered around networking strategies for penetrating the hidden job market.

Career Development and Job Search Processes

Networking plays a key role in the overall career development and job search processes. If you want to find a job or change careers, you must first know how networking relates to other equally important career development and job search steps.

Finding a job is both an art and a science; it encompasses a variety of basic facts, principles, and skills you can learn but which you must also adapt to different situations. Thus, **learning how to find a job** can be as important to career success as **knowing how to perform a job**. However, having marketable skills is essential to making job search strategies work effectively for you.

Our understanding of how to find jobs and change careers is illustrated on pages 37 and 38. As outlined on page 37, you should involve yourself in a four-step career development process as you prepare to move from one job to another:

Career Development Process

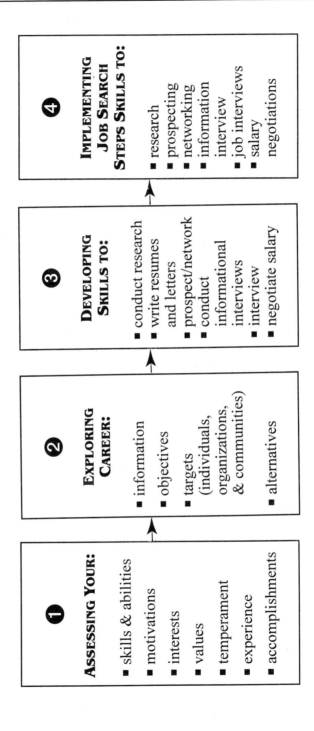

➊ ASSESSING YOUR:
- skills & abilities
- motivations
- interests
- values
- temperament
- experience
- accomplishments

➋ EXPLORING CAREER:
- information
- objectives
- targets (individuals, organizations, & communities)
- alternatives

➌ DEVELOPING SKILLS TO:
- conduct research
- write resumes and letters
- prospect/network
- conduct informational interviews
- interview
- negotiate salary

➍ IMPLEMENTING JOB SEARCH STEPS SKILLS TO:
- research
- prospecting
- networking
- information
- interview
- job interviews
- salary
- negotiations

Job Search Steps and Skills

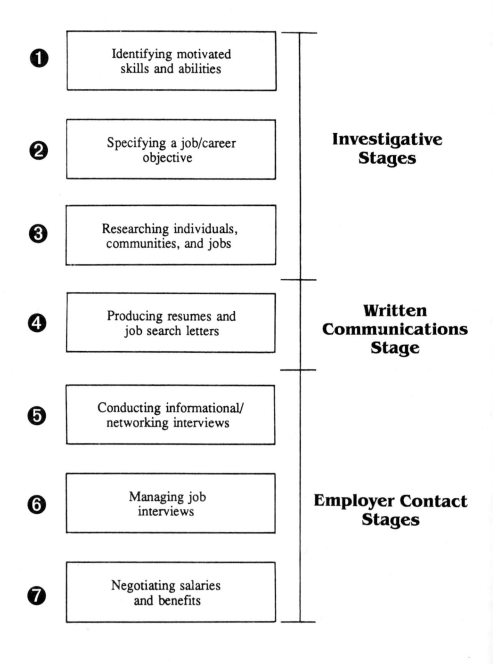

STEP 1: Conduct a self-assessment

This first step involves assessing your skills, abilities, motivations, interests, values, temperament, experience, and accomplishments. Your basic strategy is to develop a firm foundation of information about yourself before proceeding to other stages in the career development process. This self-assessment develops the necessary self-awareness upon which you can effectively communicate your qualifications to employers as well as focus and build your career.

STEP 2: Gather career information

Closely related to the first step, this second step is an exploratory, research phase of your career development. Here you need to formulate goals, gather information about alternative jobs and careers through reading and talking to informed people, and then narrow your alternatives to specific job targets.

STEP 3: Develop job search skills

The third step focuses your career around specific job search skills for landing the job you want. As further outlined on page 38, these job search skills are closely related to one another as a series of job search steps. They involve conducting research, writing resumes and letters, prospecting and networking, conducting informational interviews, interviewing for a job, and negotiating salary and terms of employment. Each of these job search skills involves well-defined strategies and tactics you must learn in order to be effective in the job market.

STEP 4: Implement each job search step

The final career development step emphasizes the importance of transforming understanding into action. You do this by implementing each job search step which already incorporates the knowledge, skills, and abilities you acquired in Steps 1, 2, and 3.

Organize and Sequence Your Job Search

The figure on page 38 further expands our career development process by examining the key elements in a successful job search. It consists of a seven-step process which relates your past, present, and future. Notice that your past is well integrated into the process of finding a job or changing your career. Therefore, you should feel comfortable conducting your job search: it represents the best of what you are in terms of your past and present accomplishments as they relate to your present and future goals. If you follow this type of job search, you will communicate your best self to employers.

Since the individual job search steps are interrelated, they should be followed in sequence. If you fail to properly complete the initial self-assessment steps, your job search may become haphazard, aimless, and costly. For example, you should never write a resume (Step 3) before first conducting an assessment of your skills (Step 1) and identifying your objective (Step 2). You normally should do networking (Step 5) after assessing your skills (Step 1), identifying your objective (Step 2), writing a resume (Step 3), and conducting research (Step 4). Indeed, relating Step 1 to Step 2 is especially critical to the successful implementation of all other job search steps. You must complete Steps 1 and 2 before continuing on to the other steps. Steps 3 to 6 can be conducted simultaneously because they complement and reinforce one another.

Try to sequence your job search as close to these steps as possible. The true value of this sequencing will become very apparent as you implement your plan.

The processes and steps identified on pages 37 and 38 represent the careering and re-careering processes we and others have used successfully with thousands of clients during the past 30 years. But this is not the complete picture on finding jobs and advancing careers in the job markets of today and tomorrow. You must do much more than just know how to find a job through networking. In the job markets of today and tomorrow, you need to constantly review your work-content skills to make sure they are appropriate for the changing job market. Once you have the necessary skills to perform jobs, you will be ready to target your skills on particular jobs and careers that you do well and enjoy doing. You will be able to avoid the trap of trying to fit into jobs that are not conducive to your particular mix of skills, motivations, and abilities.

Achieving Success Through Planning and Networking

While we recommend that you plan your job search, we want you to avoid the excesses of too much planning. Planning should not become all-consuming. Planning makes sense because it requires that you set goals and develop strategies for achieving the goals. However, too much planning can blind you to unexpected occurrences and opportunities—that wonderful experience called serendipity. Be flexible enough to take advantage of new opportunities that come your way, many of which will be generated from your networking activities.

We outline a hypothetical plan for conducting an effective job search on page 42. This plan incorporates the individual job search activities over a six-month period. If you phase in the first five job search steps during the initial three to four weeks and continue the final four steps in subsequent

> *Networking plays a central ongoing role in moving your job search to its final stages – job interviews and offers.*

weeks and months, you should begin receiving job offers within two to three months after initiating your job search. Interviews and job offers can come anytime—often unexpectedly—during your job search. The average time is within three months, but it can occur within a week or take as long as five months. If you plan, prepare, and persist at the job search, the pay-off will be job interviews and offers.

Networking plays a central ongoing role in moving your job search to its final stages—job interviews and offers. While three months may seem a long time, especially if you have just lost your job and you need work immediately, you can shorten your job search time by increasing the frequency of your prospecting, networking, and informational interviewing activities. If you are job hunting on a full-time basis, you may be able to cut your job search time in half. But don't expect to get

Organization of Job Search Activities

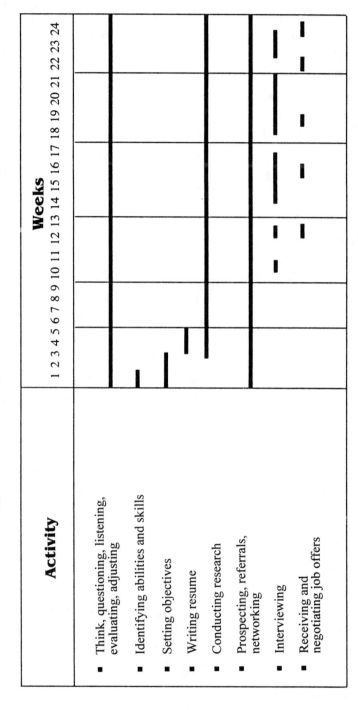

Activity	Weeks 1 2 3 4 5 6 7 8 9 10 11 12 13 14 15 16 17 18 19 20 21 22 23 24
■ Think, questioning, listening, evaluating, adjusting	
■ Identifying abilities and skills	
■ Setting objectives	
■ Writing resume	
■ Conducting research	
■ Prospecting, referrals, networking	
■ Interviewing	
■ Receiving and negotiating job offers	

a job within a week or two. It requires time and hard work—perhaps the hardest work you will ever do—but it pays off with a job that is right for you.

Do Your Homework

One word of caution before we proceed further. An important lesson we and others have learned over the years is this:

Effective networking and job interviewing are
based upon a strong job search foundation
of self-assessment, skills identification,
objective setting, research, and
resume/letter writing.

Don't short-change yourself by failing to do your homework. Build your foundation first by completing each step in the job search process. If you do this, you should become a very effective networker who will find jobs that you both do well and enjoy doing.

3

Myths and Realities

MOST PEOPLE HAVE AN IMAGE OF HOW THE JOB market works as well as how they should relate to it. This image is based upon a combination of facts, stereotypes, and myths acquired from experience and advice of well-meaning individuals. It's a useful image when it leads individuals into productive job search channels that quickly result in job interviews and offers for excellent jobs. But it's an unfortunate image when it guides people into unproductive job search channels.

Unfortunate Images and Myths

A job market image is at its worst when it advises job seekers to spend most of their time responding to vacancy announcements and waiting to hear from employers. Such an image leads job seekers into using job search approaches that often result in less than rewarding jobs. Indeed, they reconfirm the often-heard lament of the frustrated, disappointed, and unsuccessful job searcher—*"What more can I do? There are no jobs out there for me."* This should not happen to you, because you are organizing yourself as a proactive job seeker. Using networking strategies, you will take initiative to uncover numerous job leads that will result in job interviews and offers.

At the same time, there are several myths surrounding networks and networking. Like many concepts that come into vogue, this one has become the object of exaggerated claims, abuses, and misuses.

Let's examine several of these myths before you proceed to organize your networks and networking activities. Each of these myths stresses important principles for identifying, developing, expanding, and using networks and networking strategies in a job search.

Job-Search and Work-Content Skills

MYTH 1:   **Anyone can find a job; all you need to know is "how to find a job."**

REALITY: This "form versus substance" myth is often associated with career counselors who were raised on popular career planning exhortations of the 1970s and 1980s that stressed the importance of having a positive attitude and self-esteem, setting goals, dressing for success, and using interpersonal strategies for finding jobs. These individuals have been more concerned with promoting a job search philosophy—which emphasizes process skills—than with urging more job generation, the development of work-content skills, and relocation. It reflects a disturbing preference for style and image rather than substance and performance in the workplace. This myth was most likely a reality in an industrial society with low unemployment—the 1950s and 1960s—or in certain high turnover service sectors requiring low level skills—the 1980s. But it is a myth for today's post-industrial, high-tech society. In a society that requires more and more highly skilled labor, knowing how to find a job is not enough to get a good job. Getting a job in such a society also requires that (1) jobs be available (job generation), (2) individuals have the proper mix of skills to perform those jobs (work-content skills), and (3) individuals be willing to go where the jobs are located (relocation). While it is extremely important to learn job search skills, these skills are no substitute for concrete work-content skills, job generation, and relocation.

Finding Jobs

MYTH 2:   **The best way to find a job is to respond to classified ads, use employment agencies, explore online career services, submit applications, and email, fax, or mail resumes and cover letters to personnel offices.** •

REALITY: This is one of the most serious myths preventing many individuals from finding a good job. Many people do get jobs by following such formalized application and recruitment procedures. However, these are not the best ways to get the best jobs—those offering good pay, advancement opportunities, and an appropriate "fit" with one's abilities, goals, and values. This approach makes two questionable assumptions about the structure of the job market and how you should relate to it. The first assumption deals with how the job market does or should operate:

> **Assumption #1:** There exists an organized, coherent, and centralized job market "out there" where one can go to get information on available job vacancies.

In reality no such one-stop market exists. It is a highly decentralized, fragmented, and chaotic job market where job vacancy information is at best incomplete, skewed, and unrepresentative of available job opportunities at any particular moment. Classified ads, agencies, and personnel offices tend to list low paying yet highly competitive jobs. Most of the best jobs—high level, excellent pay, least competitive—are neither listed nor advertised; they are uncovered through word-of-mouth and learned about during the process of networking. When seeking employment, your most fruitful strategy will be to conduct research and informational interviews on what is called the "hidden job market"—a loosely structured network of employers and job seekers who exchange job vacancy and hiring information.

The second assumption deals with how you should relate to this job market:

Assumption #2: You should try to fit your goals and abilities into existing vacancies rather than find a job designed around your strengths.

This may be a formula for future job unhappiness. If you want to find a job fit for you rather than try to fit yourself into a job, you must use another strategy based upon a different set of assumptions regarding how you should relate your goals and abilities to the world of work.

MYTH 3: **I know how to find a job but opportunities are not available for me.**

REALITY: Most people don't know how to best find a job. They may be unable to identify work-content skills to communicate their value to employers, or they look in the wrong places where jobs are not being generated. They continue to use the most ineffective methods—responding to job listings, sending resumes, contacting employment agencies, or spending a disproportionate amount of time on the Internet looking for jobs. Opportunities are readily available for those who understand the structure and operation of the job market, can identify appropriate work-content skills, are willing to relocate, and use job search methods designed for the hidden job market. Networking is the key job search strategy for penetrating the hidden job market.

> *Networking is the key job search strategy for penetrating the hidden job market.*

MYTH 4: **One should not network in a case where there is an advertised vacancy and an employer requests a resume or completed application form.**

REALITY: Networking should especially be used in the case of advertised job vacancies. If you only complete an application form or submit a resume, chances are nothing will happen. You must take additional action—a telephone call or a personal visit—to assist your application. Such forms of networking can help your application and resume stand out from the rest.

Information, Advice, and Referrals

MYTH 5:   **The purpose of networking is to get a job interview and job offer.**

REALITY: While networking may ultimately lead to interviews and job offers, the primary purpose of networking is to get information, advice, and referrals so you can better identify job leads as well as communicate your qualifications to potential employers. In every step of your job search you need more and better information on which to make decisions; employers also need this information on potential candidates. You get this by talking to people who have information. If you approach networking as a method for getting job interviews and offers, you will most likely become ineffective. You may appear insincere and untrustworthy as you attempt to use people for personal gain. You must communicate that you are honest, sincere, likable, and competent. You can best communicate these qualities to others by seeking information, advice, and referrals.

MYTH 6:   **Networking is the key to getting a job.**

REALITY: Networking is one of several **techniques** used in getting a job. It is more or less effective depending on how you use it as well as the behavior of your intended audience. Many other methods used in finding jobs have little or nothing to do with networking: complete an application form for a job vacancy; post a resume to an online resume database; submit a letter and resume in response to a classified ad; or interview directly for a position. These traditional methods for finding a job are most appropriate for individuals who are seeking to fit their interests, experience, and qualifications into available job vacancies found on the advertised job market. Networking is most appropriate for individuals interested in finding high quality jobs that fit more directly with their own motivated abilities and skills. These jobs are more likely to be found on the hidden job market rather than on the advertised job market. Individuals who know how to network are more likely to get job interviews that lead to job offers.

> *Networking is most appropriate for individuals interested in finding high quality jobs that fit their motivated abilities and skills.*

Networking Strategies

MYTH 7:   **Your networking activities should be aimed at those who have the power to hire.**

REALITY: This belief is responsible for many abuses and misuses of networking. This is an example of how a little knowledge can become a dangerous thing. Many people who learn about networking remain confused about where to target their networking activities. They either don't know what they are doing or they lack a clear understanding about the purpose of networking. As a result, they often engage in unproductive activities. Many, for example, believe that networking is all about acquiring "connections," power, and influence in order to "pull strings" that will help get them a job. They forget that they should be **gathering high quality information and advice** in order to make employment decisions. Consequently, they only seek out people who seem to be powerful in the hopes they will open the right doors to success. Such people often pester others who are busy and have no reasons whatsoever to meet with them. Such abuses and misuses of networking are partly due to advice given to job seekers by well-meaning but inexperienced career advisors who counsel job seekers to aim their job search activities toward those who have the power to hire. Remember, networking is a communication process—exchanging information and receiving advice and referrals about jobs and careers. While it involves prospecting and informational interviewing, and it should lead to job interviews and offers, don't approach networking as strictly a job finding technique. Those that do often abuse networking by contacting individuals for the ostensible purpose of gathering information, but in reality they attempt to use the individual for getting a job. By focusing on individuals who have the power to hire, they give networking a bad name by bothering busy people who do not have the time nor interest in giving these "networkers" a job. Returning to the original purposes of networking, you will find that many people who do not have the power to hire also have very valuable information, advice, and referrals to share with you as you progress in your job search. You will find, for example, that a secretary may be able to provide greater insights into an organization—especially its politics—than more influential individuals who appear to have the power to hire. Furthermore, it is not always clear who has the power to hire, since **hiring decisions are often shared decisions** involving many individuals. Whatever you do, approach networking as a communication process rather than a process of acquiring power and influence with employers.

> *Networking is a communication process – exchanging information and receiving advice and referrals about jobs and careers.*

MYTH 8: The best way to network is to join a professional association. Members of these organizations will help you gain access to job vacancies that arise in their organizations.

REALITY: Important networking does take place in many profes-
            sional associations, but joining professional associations
            is by no means the best way to network. Indeed, too
            many people join professional associations with the mis-
            taken impression that membership alone will enhance
            their job search. Some professional associations are
            peopled by so many "networkers" looking for jobs that
            many of the more established, experienced, and talented
            professionals avoid participating in such associations for
            fear of becoming the subject of networking rather than
            participate in an organization that promotes substantive
            professional goals. Furthermore, membership in any
            organization is only as good as one's participation in the
            organization. If you decide to join professional associa-
            tions, the best form of networking is to become seen and
            known—a **participant** rather than a spectator—for your
            activities and competence within the organization. You
            should promote the goals of the organization by serving
            on committees, taking on assignments, and playing a
            significant role in monthly meetings and annual confer-
            ences. In other words, demonstrate your capabilities by
            becoming involved in the operations of the association
            rather than by collecting names, addresses, and phone
            numbers of fellow members for the misguided purpose of
            acquiring "connections" that will lead to job opportuni-
            ties. **The best form of networking is one that commu-
            nicates your qualifications to potential employers by
            demonstrating your capabilities within an organi-
            zation.**

Interpersonal and Electronic Networking

MYTH 9:   **Electronic networking is the wave of the future. It will
           largely replace interpersonal networking.**

REALITY: The two forms of networking are not mutually exclusive;
           they complement each other. Indeed, a great deal of hype
           surrounds the Internet job search, which primarily
           involves the application of computer technology to the
           recruitment and job search processes. The technology

helps speed communication between job seekers and employers as well as helps each group better locate and screen each other. Without questioning effectiveness, many job seekers get the false impression that jobs can best be found on the Internet or through various electronic job banks and online career services. Many of them only use online services for posting their resumes and reviewing jobs listings. Such an impression and resulting behavior may dissuade many job seekers from using what may prove to be more effective interpersonal networking techniques. The best part of electronic networking is the use of email for transmitting messages,

> **When you use email for networking purposes, you go online to make connections, build relationships, and nurture your network.**

letters, resumes, and other forms of job search communication. When you use email for networking purposes, you go online to make connections, build relationships, and nurture your network. In so doing, the results should be similar to offline networking—you acquire information, advice, and referrals that lead to job interviews and offers. Employment websites, such as Monster.com, that include message boards and chat groups operated by career experts and visited by employers and fellow job seekers, can yield useful information, advice, and referrals for making connections and building relationships which lie at the heart of the networking process. Most online employment services allow employers to cut recruitment costs by searching for candidates—inexpensive alternatives to placing classified ads and using executive search firms. Most of these services are shaped by the needs of employers, because employers are the ones who directly support these services. While the resume database and job listing components of online employment services increasingly play an important role in the employment process, be sure to use the networking component of these services. The central problem remains communication between employers and job seekers. You are well advised to perfect both your off-line and online networking skills. This means becoming a savvy communicator by mail, fax, and email. It also means becoming a savvy Internet user who knows how to find the best places online to network for job information, advice, and referrals.

Resumes and Networking

MYTH 10:   **One should network rather than use resumes and letters for finding a job.**

REALITY: Networking is no substitute for the more traditional means of communicating your qualifications to employers—resumes and letters. Again, confusion often arises over the purpose and role of both resumes and networking in the job search. During certain stages of one's job search, resumes and letters must be written and disseminated by mail, fax, or email. This occurs after identifying one's motivated abilities and setting an objective. Resumes may be used to help uncover job leads, and networking helps identify to whom to send resumes and letters. At the same time, resumes and letters play an important role in the

> *Always keep copies of your resume close to you. You never know when you will use them as part of your networking activities.*

networking process. The resume, for example, should be presented at the very end of an informational interview for the purpose of receiving advice on how to improve its content as well as for summarizing your goals, experience, and qualifications. You will want your networking contact to **refer you and your resume to others** who might be interested in your job search and qualifications. At the same time, you must write different types of letters as part of your networking campaign. To conduct a job search or engage in networking activities without a powerful one- or two-page resume, or without using referral and thank-you letters, is simply foolish. Always keep copies of your resume close to you. You never know when you will use them as part of your networking activities.

Resumes and Informational Interviews

MYTH 11: **I should send a resume with my approach letter when initiating a networking contact.**

REALITY: Never, never, never send a resume to a contact unless the individual requests it. Remember, the purpose of networking is to get information, advice, and referrals relevant to uncovering job leads and interviews. The resume should only be revealed at the end of the informational interview—for a critique.

Informational Interviews

MYTH 12: **In the informational interview, you want to impress upon the interviewer that you are qualified for a job.**

REALITY: The informational interview is an important means of (1) exchanging information about job alternatives relevant to your interests, experience, and qualifications; (2) learning how to strengthen your job search; and (3) receiving referrals for expanding your networks. In an informational interview, you are the interviewer and the other person is the interviewee. Interviewers need not impress their qualifications on interviewees unless they are confused as to whom is conducting the interview and for what purpose.

Rejections

MYTH 13: **You will seldom be rejected for an informational interview.**

REALITY: This is true if you approach the informational interview properly. However, if you (1) only focus on persons who have the power to hire, and (2) attempt to use the informational interview to get job interviews and offers, you may experience many rejections. Few people are interested in assisting others who primarily want to use them for personal gain.

Initiating Contacts

MYTH 14:   **The best way to initiate contacts for networking is to write a letter requesting an informational interview.**

REALITY: While letters play an important role in a job search if written and used properly, a telephone call is likely to be more effective because you will receive immediate feedback and you will be initially screened for the informational interview.

Referrals

MYTH 15:   **It is always best to use referrals when networking.**

REALITY: Referrals are important in making contacts, but they are not necessarily the best way to proceed. Referrals help ease the process of introducing oneself to strangers, and they build on relationships of others. However, too much emphasis is often placed on referrals to the detriment of taking individual initiative in establishing cold contacts. Indeed, you may do just as well on your own by making contacts with strangers. The problem with referrals is twofold: (1) they are often time consuming because they rely too much on personal relationships, and (2) you cannot be certain of the nature of the relationship between the sources of your referral and your networking contact, i.e., whether it is positive or negative for you. Cold calling techniques can be more effective because they can be initiated rapidly and do not involve a questionable third-party relationship. However, for shy individuals who have difficulty making cold contacts, the referral method will be easier, and they will receive few rejections.

Long-Distance Networking

MYTH 16:   **Networking does not work well when you attempt to conduct a job search in an unfamiliar community. In such cases it is best to respond to vacancy announcements, contact employment agencies, or send resumes and letters directly to prospective employers.**

REALITY: Networking is not limited to the community in which you live. It can work anywhere, if you know what you are doing and can develop an effective long-distance job search campaign. If you are targeting your job search on another community, it is best to develop both individual and organizational contacts by telephone, email, and personal visits to the community. While you may have to rely more on cold calling techniques, the techniques should work well if you spend the proper amount of time using them to uncover informational interviewing leads.

Cooperation

MYTH 17:   **Most people are reluctant to share information about their job or career.**

REALITY: Most people, regardless of their position or status, love to talk about their work and give advice to both friends and strangers. You can learn the most about job opportunities and alternative careers by talking to such people through your networking activities.

Approaching Strangers

MYTH 18:   **I'm too shy to approach strangers through either referrals or cold calls. I'm just not assertive enough. I'm especially afraid of being rejected.**

REALITY: You need not be overly assertive in the process of networking. There are many effective techniques that can help overcome shyness. Best of all, the process of networking is aimed at **sharing information**—something that does not require assertiveness nor involve stress commonly associated with shyness. Since you are not asking for a job and thus not putting others in an uncomfortable position of considering you for a job, you will encounter few rejections in the process of networking.

Planning and Luck

MYTH 19:   **You can plan all you want, but getting a job is really a function of good luck.**

REALITY: Luck is more than just chance. Above all, luck in the job search is a function of being in the right place at the right time to take advantage of opportunities that come your way. Therefore, the best way to have luck come your way is to **plan to be in many different places at many different times**. You do this by putting together an excellent resume and network with it in both the advertised and hidden job markets. If you are persistent in implementing your plans, luck may strike you many times!

Additional Realities

You will encounter several other realities in the process of developing your networks and networking for information, advice, and referrals. Among these are the following:

REALITY: **You will find less competition for high-level jobs than for middle- and low-level jobs.**

                     Hiring procedures for middle- and low-level jobs tend to be more formalized, requiring resumes and application forms, because of the high competition for these jobs. As a result, networking may be less effective for these levels of employment. Competition is generally less keen for higher-level positions where hiring procedures are less formalized. It is at this level where networking may be more effective.

REALITY: **Your networks and networking activities might include individuals in personnel offices, but don't expect them to be in control of hiring decisions.**

Personnel offices primarily screen candidates for employers who are found in operating units of organizations. Knowing this, you should expand your job search efforts toward those who are more directly involved in the actual hiring process.

REALITY: **Politics are both ubiquitous and dangerous in many organizations.**

If you think you are above politics, you may quickly become one of its victims. Unfortunately, you only learn about "local politics" **after** you accept a position and begin relating to the different players in the organization. It is wise to learn about the internal politics of an organization prior to accepting a position. You can do this most effectively through your networking activities.

REALITY: **It is best to narrow in or "rifle" your job search on particular organizations and individuals rather than broaden or "shotgun" it to many alternatives.**

Your networking activities increasingly require you to conduct a well organized and focused job search. While initially you may not have a clear idea of what you want to do and where you hope to do it, the more you network and conduct informational interviews, the more you should become focused on specific career goals and organizations. If you fail to focus your job search, you will most likely present a confused image to your network contacts as well as to potential employers.

REALITY: **Employment firms, personnel agencies, and online employment services may not be helpful in your job search.**

Most employment firms, personnel agencies, and online employment services work for employers and themselves rather than for applicants. Few have your best interests at heart. Use them only after you have investigated their effectiveness. Avoid firms that require up-front money for a promise of performance. In the end your best friend in finding a job will be **you** and your own well organized job search centered around networking activities.

REALITY: **Most people can make satisfying job and career changes.**

If you minimize efforts in the advertised job market and concentrate instead on planning and implementing a well organized job search tailored to the realities of the hidden job market, you should be successful in making a job or career change that is most compatible with your interests, skills, and experience.

REALITY: **"Connections" or "pull" can be very effective in finding a job or changing careers.**

Many employers welcome informal contacts with candidates who are connected to friends, relatives, and acquaintances. Such connections perform an important function within the job market: they provide basic screening of individuals by those who know the candidate. Such screening is preferable to much of the screening information acquired from the formal hiring process —letters of recommendations, interviews, and conversations with former employers. A personal contact, acquired through networking, often provides more reliable and trusted information about candidates than information received from strangers who frequently have a vested interest in accentuating the positives rather than revealing the negatives of former employees.

Prepare For Advice and Chaos

As you conduct your job search and networking activities, you will encounter many of these and other myths and realities about how you should relate to the job market. Several people will give you advice. While much of this advice will be useful, a great deal of it will be useless and misleading. You should be skeptical of well-meaning individuals who most likely will reiterate the same job and career myths. You should be particularly leery of those who try to **sell** you their advice.

Your task is to organize the chaos around your skills and interests. Networking will help you do this.

Always remember you are entering a relatively disorganized and chaotic job market which has the appearance of organization and coherence. If you approach this job market properly, you will encounter numerous and exciting job opportunities. Your task is to organize the chaos around your skills and interests. You must convince prospective employers that they will like you more than other "qualified" candidates. Networking should play a key role in organizing the job market and communicating your qualifications to employers.

4

Build Your Network

YOUR NETWORK MAY BE YOUR MOST PRIZED YET neglected resource for finding a job or changing careers. *"Whom you know"* and *"Who knows you"* are likely to be just as important to finding a job as *"What you can do."* You must first identify who defines your current network before you can develop, expand, and use networks in the job search process through the use of prospecting, networking, and informational interviewing techniques.

Identify Your Network

Everyone has a network whether they realize it or not. It consists of individuals they know and interact with and who influence each other's behavior. Perhaps you regularly meet with 10 people on a daily basis. These individuals may constitute the most important **members** in your network: spouse, children, neighbors, boss, fellow workers, professional colleagues, friends, and acquaintances. You **know** their characteristics, how they behave, and to what degree they relate to you. You have **expectations** concerning how these individuals will behave toward you, and they have expectations about how you will relate to them. You **play different roles**, depending on whom you interact with. During much of the day you may play the roles of employee, supervisor, and colleague, but during other times of the day you may perform the roles of spouse, parent, friend, neighbor, and/or customer.

At the same time, individuals defining your network also have expectations that influence your own behavior. Your work habits, for example, may include arriving at work five minutes early each day. You do this because your supervisor expects you to be punctual, and you believe it's important to impress upon both your supervisor and co-workers the importance of punctuality. Individuals in your network know you as someone who usually plays a specific role vis-a-vis them-selves: spouse, father, supervisor, colleague, friend, or acquaintance. Seldom do you present yourself to the same individual in more than one role.

You know many other individuals whom you may or may not interact with on a regular basis. For example, you have relatives that you may see only once a year; an old high school friend you still exchange Christmas cards with; a sorority sister you haven't seen in over seven years; a former high school or college teacher; or your doctor, lawyer, banker, insurance agent, and minister whom you only occasionally meet. While not as important to you on a daily basis, many of these individuals may play critical roles during certain times of your life. All should be included in your network.

Develop a Contact List

One of the best ways to identify members in your network is to develop a contact list. Begin by making a list of 200 people you know. This list will most likely include relatives, neighbors, fellow workers, former employers, alumni, friends, acquaintances, bankers, doctors, lawyers, ministers, and professional colleagues. Perhaps only 10 of these people will be in your immediate day-to-day network. The others may be former friends, acquaintances, or your Aunt Betsy whom you haven't seen in over 10 years. If you have difficulty developing such a list, refresh your memory by referring to the following checklist of categories:

Categories For Contact List

❑   Friends (consult your Christmas card list)

❑   Neighbors (past and present)

❑ Social acquaintances (group and club members)

❑ Classmates (high school and college)

❑ Local alumni

❑ People you consulted or wrote a check to during the past 12 months:

    ❑ tradespeople, drugstore owner

    ❑ doctor, dentist, optician, therapist

    ❑ lawyer, accountant, real estate agent

    ❑ insurance agent, stock broker, travel agent

❑ Local bank manager

❑ Relatives (immediate and distant)

❑ Politicians (local, state, and national)

❑ Chamber of Commerce members

❑ Pastors, ministers

❑ Church members

❑ Trade association members

❑ Professional organization executives

❑ Other members of professional organizations

❑ People you meet at conferences or conventions

❑ Speakers at meetings you've attended

❑ Business club executives and members (Rotary, Kiwanis, Jaycees, etc.)

❑ Representatives of direct-sales businesses (real estate, insurance, Amway, Shaklee, Avon)

❑ Other

After developing your comprehensive list of contacts, classify the names into four different categories:

- Those in influential positions or who have hiring authority.
- Those with job leads.
- Those most likely to refer you to others.
- Those with long-distance contacts.

Select at least 25 individuals from your list of 200 names for initiating your first round of contacts. You are now ready to begin an active prospecting and networking campaign which will enable you to expand your present network considerably by linking it to others' networks. This campaign should lead to informational interviews, formal job interviews, and job offers.

Expand Your Network

Methods for expanding one's networks are closely related to several face-to-face sales techniques used in the insurance, real estate, and other direct-sales businesses: prospecting, pyramiding, and client referral systems. In the job search the analogous techniques become **prospecting**, **networking**, and **informational interviewing**. Your job search goals and situations will be similar to those found in many successful businesses:

- Your goal is to sell an important high quality product— yourself—by shopping around for a good buyer—an employer.

- The buyer wants to be assured, based upon previous and current demonstration, that he or she is investing in a high quality and reliable product.

- Face-to-face communication, rather than impersonal advertising, remains the best way to make buying/selling decisions.

- When the buyer and seller exchange information about each other, the quality of information improves and the new relationship will probably be mutually beneficial, and satisfying.

The job search techniques of prospecting, networking, and informational interviewing are relatively easy to learn and use. However, you must first understand the nature of networks, pyramids, and referral systems used in sales. As noted earlier, a network consists of you and people you know, who are important to you, and with whom you interact most frequently. Many of these people influence your behavior. Others may also influence your behavior but you interact with them less frequently. As illustrated earlier on page 21, your network may consist of family, friends, assisters, professional colleagues, fellow workers, and your supervisor. Your network of relationships involves **people**—not data, things, or knowledge of a particular subject area—who may provide you with the most critical assistance in your job search—information, advice, and referrals.

Build Networks Through Prospecting

The key to successful networking is an active and routine **prospecting campaign**. Salespersons in insurance, real estate, Amway, Shaklee, and other direct-sales businesses understand the importance and principles of prospecting; indeed, many have turned the art of prospecting into a science!

Prospecting is conducted by means of emails, letters, telephone calls, faxes, and face-to-face meetings. The quickest way to generate numerous prospects is to use the **telephone**. The degree of effectiveness, however, depends on whether you initiate the call based on a referral or make a cold call. The cold call is the least effective prospecting method, but it is very efficient and thus generates a much larger volume of contacts than any other prospecting method. **Emails and letters** require follow-up—preferably by telephone—to be effective. While **face-to-face meetings** will be your most effective prospecting method, such meetings are very time consuming; they will cut down on the overall efficiency of your prospecting campaign.

> *The key to successful networking is an active and routine prospecting campaign which operates according to the principle of probability.*

The basic operating principle behind prospecting techniques is **probability**: the number of sales you make is a direct function of the amount of effort you put into developing new contacts and following through. Expect no more than a 10-percent acceptance rate: for every 10 people you contact, nine will reject you and one will accept you. Therefore, the more people you contact, the more acceptances you will receive. If you want to be successful, you must collect many more "nos" than "yeses." In a 10-percent probability situation, you need to contact 100 people for 10 successes.

These prospecting principles are extremely useful for your job search. Like sales situations, the job search is a highly ego-involved activity often characterized by numerous rejections accompanied by a few acceptances. While no one wants to be rejected, few people are willing and able to handle more than a few rejections. They take a "no" as a sign of personal failure—and quit prematurely. If they persisted longer, they would achieve success after a few more "nos." Furthermore, if their prospecting activities were focused on **gathering information** rather than making sales, they would considerably minimize the number of rejections they receive.

Knowing these probabilistic negative and positive outcomes of most prospecting campaigns, your best approach to prospecting in a job search is to:

- **Prospect** for job leads.

- **Accept rejections** as part of the game.

- **Link prospecting** to networking and informational interviewing.

- **Keep prospecting** for more "yeses," contacts, information, advice, and referrals that will eventually translate into job interviews and offers.

Prospecting involves contacting people in your network and building new networks for information and job leads. Many people in direct-sales quit at this point because they lack the prerequisites for success—patience, perseverance, and a positive attitude. Prospecting techniques require you to:

- Develop enthusiastic one-on-one appointments and informational interview presentations.

- Be consistent and persistent in how you present your case.

- Give prospecting and follow-up high priorities in your overall daily routine.

- Believe you will be successful given your persistence with these techniques; prospecting is a probability game involving both successes and failures.

Make Many Contacts

A good prospecting pace to begin with is to make two new contacts each day. Start by contacting people in your immediate network. Let them know you are conducting a job search, but emphasize that you are only doing research. Ask for a few moments of their time to discuss your information needs. You are only seeking **information and advice** at this time—not a job.

Prospecting and networking, above all, requires **persistence**. For example, it takes about 20 minutes to initiate a contact by telephone— longer by letter. If you contact at least one person in your immediate circle of contacts each day, your prospecting should yield 15 new contacts each week for a total investment of less than two hours. Each of these new contacts could possibly yield three additional contacts or 45 new referrals. However, some contacts will yield more than three and others may yield none. If you develop contacts in this manner, you will create a series of small pyramids or networks, as illustrated on page 68. If you expand your prospecting from one to three new contacts each day, you could generate 135 new contacts and referrals in a single week. If you continue this same level of activity over a two-month period, it is possible to create over 1,000 new contacts and referrals! At this pace, your odds of uncovering job opportunities, being invited to formal job interviews, and receiving job offers will increase dramatically.

The more contacts you make, the more useful information, advice, and job leads you will receive. If your job search bogs down, you probably need to increase your prospecting activities. Indeed, the single most important reason for slow and ineffective job searches that result in complaints that *"there are no jobs out there for me"* is the failure to conduct an active and persistent prospecting campaign that leads to referrals and informational interviews.

The linkages and pyramids on page 68 constitute your **job search network**. Always remember to nurture and manage this network so it performs well in generating information and job leads. As you follow through on making new contacts, expect about half to result in referrals. However, a few of your contacts will continue to give you referrals beyond the initial ones. Consequently, **you need to continually develop**

Developing Networks Through Daily Prospecting

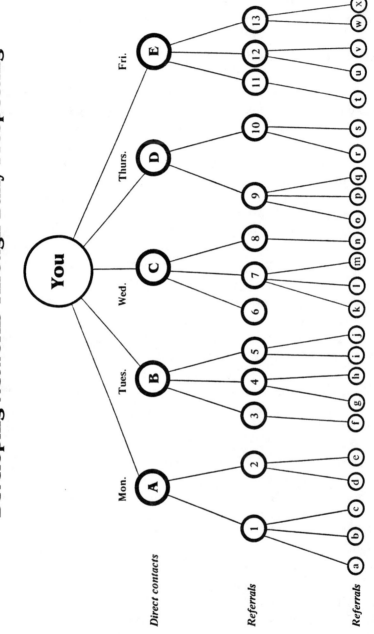

new contacts while maintaining communication with prior contacts. When conducting informational interviews, as we will see shortly, ask your contacts to keep you in mind if they hear of anyone who might be interested in your qualifications.

While prospecting is an excellent way to create contacts, it also helps you develop a realistic objective, effective interview skills, and self-confidence. In using this system, you will seldom be turned down for an informational interview. You should uncover vacancies on the hidden job market as well as place yourself in a positive position to take advantage of such opportunities.

Never directly ask for a job while prospecting, networking, and conducting informational interviews. Asking for a job puts your contact under pressure; it is the quickest way to be politely shown the door. The basic principle behind networking is this: The best way to get a job is never ask for a job directly; always ask for information, advice, and referrals. By doing

> *The best way to get a job is never ask for a job directly; always ask for information, advice, and referrals.*

this, you will be interviewed, your resume will be read, and, if you listen to the advice you receive, you eventually will be offered a job through one or more of your contacts.

Our prospecting system is similar to the networking techniques used in the direct-sales businesses. These proven, low-keyed sales techniques require persistence, a personable approach to people, and the ability to share a "product" and offer an opportunity to prospective buyers. This low stress approach does not threaten individuals by asking them to buy something, or, in your case, give you a job. Some of the most successful businesses in the world have been built on this simple one-on-one prospecting, networking, and referral strategy. When adapted to the job search process, the same strategies have resulted in extremely successful job placements.

Telephone For Job Leads

Telephone communication plays an important role in prospecting, networking, and informational interviewing activities. However, controversy centers around how and when to use the telephone in prospecting for job leads and generating informational interviewing. Some people recommend writing a letter and waiting for a written or telephone reply. Others suggest writing a letter and following it with a telephone call. Still others argue you should use the telephone exclusively rather than write letters.

How you use the telephone will indicate what type of job search you are conducting. Exclusive reliance on the telephone is a technique used by highly formalized job clubs which operate phone banks for generating job leads. Using the Yellow Pages or Internet phone directories as the guide to employers, a job club member may call as many as 50 employers a day to schedule interviews. A rather aggressive yet typical telephone dialogue goes something like this:

> *"Hello, my name is Jim Baker. I would like to speak to the head of the training department. By the way, what is the name of the training director?"*

> *"You want to talk to Ms. Stevens. Her number is 723-8191, or do you want me to connect you?"*

> *"Hello, Ms. Stevens. This is Jim Baker. I have several years of training experience as both a trainer and developer of training materials. I would like to meet with you to discuss possible openings in your department for someone with my qualifications. Would it be possible to see you on Friday at 2pm?"*

Not surprising, this telephone approach generates many *"nos."* If you have a hard time handling rejections, this telephone approach will help you confront your anxieties. The principle behind this approach is **probability**: for every 25 telephone *"nos"* you receive, you will probably get one or two *"yeses."* Success is just 25 telephone calls away! If you start calling prospective employers at 9am and finish your 12 calls by noon, you should generate at least one or two interviews. That's not bad for three hours of job search work. It beats sending out letters.

The telephone is more efficient than writing letters. However, its effectiveness is questionable. When you use the telephone in this manner, you are basically asking for a job. You are asking the employer: *"Do you have a job for me?"* There is nothing subtle or particularly professional about this approach. It is effective in uncovering particular types of job leads for particular types of individuals. If you need any job in a hurry, this is one of the most efficient ways of finding employment. It's much better than standing in line at the state employment office! But if you are more concerned with finding a job that is right for you—a job you do well and enjoy doing, one that is fit for you—this telephone approach may be inappropriate.

You must use your own judgment in determining when and how to use the telephone for prospecting and networking purposes. As we've outlined elsewhere (***Dynamite Tele-Search***, Impact Publications), there are appropriate times and methods for using the telephone, and these should relate to your job search goals and needs. For example, you must be prepared to handle a formidable gatekeeper in today's telephone communication—voice mail. You'll also need to develop appealing telephone scripts that generate positive responses to your telephone inquiries and increase your overall networking effectiveness. We'll review these techniques with sample telephone dialogues in Chapter 5.

> *The telephone is more efficient than writing letters. However, its effectiveness is questionable.*

For most job seekers, the more conventional approach of writing a letter followed by a telephone call can work well in building networks. While you take the initiative in scheduling an appointment, you do not put the individual on the spot by asking for a job. You are only seeking information, advice, and referrals. This low-keyed approach results in numerous acceptances and has a higher probability of paying off with interviews than the aggressive telephone request. You should be trying to uncover jobs that are right for you rather than any job that happens to pop up from a telephoning blitz.

Minimize Rejections

These prospecting and networking methods are effective. While they are responsible for building, maintaining, and expanding multi-million dollar businesses, they work extremely well for job hunters. But they only work if you are patient and persist. The key to networking success is to focus on gathering information while also learning to handle rejections. Learn from rejections, forget them, and go on to more productive networking activities. The major reason direct-sales people fail is because they don't persist. The reason they don't persist is because they either can't take, or get tired of taking, rejections.

Rejections are no fun, especially in such an ego-involved activity as a job search. But you will encounter rejections as you travel on the road toward job search success. This road is strewn with individuals who quit prematurely because they were rejected four or five times. Don't be one of them!

Our prospecting and networking techniques differ from sales approaches in one major respect: we have special techniques for minimizing the number of rejections. If handled properly, at least 50 percent—maybe as many as 90 percent—of your prospects will turn into *"yeses"* rather than *"nos."* The reason for this unusually high acceptance rate is how you introduce and handle yourself before your prospects. Many insurance agents and direct distributors expect a 90 percent rejection rate, because they are trying to sell specific products potential clients may or may not need. Most people don't like to be put on the spot—especially when it is in their own home or office—to make a decision to buy a product.

> **The key to networking success is to focus on gathering information while also learning to handle rejections.**

Be Honest and Sincere

The principles of selling yourself in the job market are similar. People don't want to be put on the spot. They feel uncomfortable if they think you expect them to give you a job. Thus, you should never introduce yourself to a prospect by asking them for a job or a job lead. You should do just the opposite: relieve their anxiety by mentioning that you are not looking for a job from them—only job information and advice. You must be honest and sincere in communicating these intentions to your contact. The biggest turn-off for individuals targeted for informational interviews is insincere job seekers who try to use this as a mechanism to get a job.

Your approach to prospects must be subtle, honest, and professional. You are seeking information, advice, and referrals in several of these areas:

- Job opportunities
- Your job search approach
- Your resume
- Others who may have similar information, advice, and referrals.

Most people willingly volunteer such information. They generally like to talk about themselves, their careers, and others. They like to give advice. This approach flatters individuals by placing them in the role of the expert-advisor. Who doesn't want to be recognized as an expert-advisor, especially on such a critical topic as one's employment?

This approach should yield a great deal of information, advice, and referrals from your prospects. One other important outcome should result form using this approach: people will **remember** you as the person who made them feel at ease and who received their valuable advice. If they hear of job opportunities for someone with your qualifications, chances are they will contact you with the information. After contacting 100 prospects, you will have created 100 sets of eyes and ears to help you in your job search!

Observe the 5R's of Informational Interviewing

When you engage your prospects in the informational interviewing process, you want them to engage in the 5R's of informational interviewing:

- **Reveal** useful information and advice.
- **Refer** you to others for additional information and advice.
- **Read** and **revise** your resume.
- **Remember** you for future reference.

If you follow these principles, you should join the ranks of thousands of successful job seekers who paid a great deal of money learning these same principles from highly paid professionals. Save your money by **implementing** the principles outlined here.

5

Develop Job Leads and Conduct Interviews

WHILE PROSPECTING IS THE MOST IMPORTANT technique for expanding your networks, the informational interview is the major networking method used for conducting an effective job search. Again, your goal is to get information, advice, and referrals that may turn into job leads and interviews. You do this by developing a very effective informational interviewing approach to individuals in your expanded network.

Employers' Needs

Put yourself in the position of an employer again for a moment. Your problem is how to go about filling a job vacancy. If you advertise the position, you may be bombarded with hundreds of applications, phone calls, faxes, emails, and walk-ins. While you do want to hire the best qualified individual for the job, you simply don't have the time nor patience to review scores of applications. Even if you use a P.O. Box number, the paperwork may be overwhelming. Furthermore, with limited information from application forms, cover letters, and resumes, you find it hard to identify the best qualified individuals to invite for an interview; indeed, many candidates look the same on paper!

So what do you do? How can you best cut through this process? You might hire a professional job search firm to take on all of this additional work. On the other hand, you may want to better control the hiring process. Like many other employers, you begin by calling your friends, acquaintances, and other business associates and ask if they or someone else might know of any good candidates for the position. If they can't help, you ask them to give you a call should they learn of anyone qualified for your vacancy. You, in effect, create your own hidden job market—an informal information network for locating desirable candidates. Your trusted contacts initially screen the candidates in the process of referring them to you.

Informational Interviews

Based on this understanding of the employer's perspective, what should you do to best improve your chances of getting an interview and job offer? Remember, the employer needs to solve a personnel problem. By **networking** and **conducting informational interviews**, you help the employer solve his or her problem by giving him a chance to examine what you can offer him. You gain several advantages by conducting these interviews:

- You are less likely to encounter rejections since you are not asking for a job—only information, advice, referrals, and to be remembered.

- You go after higher level positions.

- You encounter little competition.

- You go directly to the people who have influence in the hiring process.

- You are likely to be invited to job interviews based upon the referrals you receive.

This job search approach has a much higher probability of generating job interviews and offers than the more traditional shotgunning and advertised job market approaches.

While you will encounter some *"nos"* in your search for *"yeses,"* informational interviews minimize the number of *"nos"* you will collect. Using this approach, you seldom will be turned down for an interview. In fact, most people will be happy to share their experiences with you and give you information, advice, and referrals. Most important, informational interviews help you overcome the likelihood of rejection.

The first rule in conducting informational interviews is to never ask for a job. When you ask for a job, or ask to be interviewed for a job (which you do when you send off your resume), you set yourself up to receive a rejection. If no job is available, you put the employer in an uncomfortable position of telling you *"no."* If you apply for an advertised opening, you will probably get lost in the herd of applicants. On the other hand, if you request an interview for information and advice—not a job—you are likely to get a *"yes."*

> **The first rule in conducting informational interviews is to never ask for a job.**

Informational interviews will help you build networks for locating the better jobs and careers. For example, look at the classifieds in your local newspaper. Most of the positions listed are either lower level positions, or they require a high level of technical skills —in other words, positions that are difficult to fill. Since the jobs you learn about through your networks are often neither advertised nor competitive, your odds of getting a good job improve considerably. As you continue making new contacts through additional referrals, you will build a large network of job contacts. Individuals in your network will be your eyes and ears for locating job opportunities that are appropriate to your goals and skills.

Enter the Back Door

Regardless of what you have heard about affirmative action, equal opportunity, the need to advertise positions, classified ads, and online job postings, the unadvertised or hidden job market still exists and continues to thrive. It is not our intent to sit in judgment of what should or should not be proper employment behavior. Rather, our job is to help you understand the realities of today's job market and prepare you to handle these realities to your maximum advantage.

Suffice it to say that you can gain access to most jobs through both a front door and a back door. Long lines normally form at the front door. If you conduct informational interviews and network, you should be able to enter through the back door. Job seekers find this entrance infinitely more responsive and rewarding than standing in line. You, too, may wish to join the successful job seekers who know how to get through the door to see the person who has the power to hire.

Your information/networking interviews help you bypass personnel offices and other gatekeepers who lack the power to hire. Personnel offices have many functions, but they seldom hire. They advertise positions, take applications, and administer tests; many also conduct initial screening interviews. The hiring function usually rests with the department head/manager for mid-level positions; upper management hires for senior upper-level positions. One of your initial job search tasks should be to identify who makes the hiring decision in the organizations for which you seek employment. Once you have this information, you'll be in a better position to effectively target your networking activities.

Approach the Right People

Whom should you contact within an organization for an informational interview? It is difficult to give one best answer to this question. Ideally you should contact people who are busy, who have the power to hire, and who are knowledgeable about the organization. The least likely candidate will be someone in the personnel department. Most often the heads of operating units are the most busy, powerful, and knowledgeable individuals in the organization. However, getting access to such individuals may be difficult. At the same time, some people at the top may appear to be informed and powerful, but they may lack information on the day-to-day personnel changes, or their influence is limited in the hiring process.

> *Aim for the busy, powerful, and informed, but be prepared to settle for less.*

We recommend contacting a variety of people. Aim for the busy, powerful, and informed, but be prepared to settle for less. Secretaries, receptionists, and the person you want to meet may refer you to others. From a practical standpoint, you may have to take whomever you can schedule an appointment with. Sometimes people who are not busy can be helpful. Talk to a secretary or receptionist sometime about working in the organization. You may be surprised by what you learn!

Nonetheless, you will conduct informational interviews with different types of people. Some will be friends, relatives, or acquaintances. Others will be referrals or new contacts. You will gain the easiest access to people you already know. This can usually be done informally by telephone. You might meet at their home or office or at a restaurant.

Use the Telephone Frequently and Effectively

Don't expect to conduct all of your informational interviews in person. To do so is expecting too much from busy people and may be naive given the busy nature of communication these days. Be prepared to conduct many networking activities over the telephone rather than in face-to-face settings. It is both to your advantage and others to do so. Busy people often prefer using the telephone to scheduling meetings. The quality of information you receive over the telephone may even be better than in face-to-face meetings since telephone conversations are less inhibited than those taking place in face-to-face settings. In fact, nearly 80 percent of all your networking activities can be conveniently conducted over the telephone.

Nearly 80 percent of all your networking activities can be conveniently conducted over the telephone.

Effective telephone communication is easier said than done. Many people, for example, are reluctant to pick up the telephone to initiate contacts with strangers. They feel uncomfortable and awkward, afraid they will say the wrong things or make fools of themselves. This should not happen to you since you may quickly find that your telephone is your best networking friend.

Telephone networking should play a central role in your job search. The telephone is an extremely efficient way to quickly acquire useful information, make job contacts, and schedule job interviews. A few simple telephone techniques should put you on the right road to becoming a effective telephone networker. Here are few examples of how you can initiate both cold calls and referral interviews over the telephone:

Cold Call for Contact Information

CALLER: *"Hi. This is Terri Bays. I'm trying to contact the person in charge of marketing. Who would that be?"*

RECEIVER: *"That's Eric Walton. He's the Director."*

CALLER: *"I need to contact him about some marketing concerns. Does he have a direct number or an extension number?"*

RECEIVER: *"His number is 281-7821. Should I transfer you?"*

ANALYSIS: This is a straightforward call for information. It follows the basic *"I'm X, who's Y, and how do I reach Y?"* format. Most gatekeepers volunteer this information with few questions asked—if you mention that you have "business" to conduct.

Cold Call With Message

CALLER: *"This is Terri Bays calling for Eric Walton."*

RECEIVER: *"Mr. Walton is in a meeting at present. Would you like to leave a message?"*

CALLER: *"Yes. Could you tell him Terri Bays called. My number is 731-3000. I would like to speak with him concerning his work in . . . . I'll be in my office the rest of the day as well as between 9:00am and 4:00pm tomorrow. Thank you."*

ANALYSIS: The caller immediately identifies herself and requests to speak with the person. Given this direct *"I'm X calling for Y"* approach, the gatekeeper may assume you know the person and thus be more willing to field your call. When making such a cold call, you should leave a complete message in which you (1) state your name, (2) leave your phone number, (3) indicate the nature of your business, and (4) identify your availability during the next 24 hours for a return call. Whether or not you receive a return call depends in part on the quality of your message concerning the nature of your business. Leave enough information that will motivate the person to return your call—not too much nor too little. The same message should be left if the person is immediately reached by voice mail or the gatekeeper puts you through to a voice mailbox.

Cold Call Screened By Gatekeeper

CALLER: *"This is Terri Bays calling for Eric Walton."*

RECEIVER: *"Where are you calling from and what is the nature of your business?"*

CALLER: *"I'm calling from Indianapolis. I would like to speak with Mr. Walton about his work in . . ."*

RECEIVER: *"Let me check to see if he is available."*

Cold Call Making Direct Contact

CALLER: *"This is Terri Bays calling for Eric Walton."*

RECEIVER: *"Speaking."*

CALLER: *"I'm calling about your work in marketing. I'm in the process of gathering information on opportunities in international marketing and thought you could be a good person to talk with because of your extensive experience with Bellows International. Do you have a few minutes or would it be better if I called back at a more convenient time?"*

RECEIVER: *"I'm really not sure I can be of much help. I'm very busy right now. What type of information do you need?"*

CALLER: *"I recently completed my Bachelor's degree in International Marketing at Indiana University. I speak Russian and have traveled extensively throughout Eastern Europe. I really want to start my career in this fascinating part of the world, but I'm not sure how to best proceed at this point. I'm now gathering information on pharmaceutical companies that have begun marketing their products in Russia and the Newly Independent States. Since I know you've done extensive international marketing, do you know who the major players are in this region? I'm trying to identify four* *or five of the key companies that are either currently in the area or interested in expanding their operations there."*

ANALYSIS: The caller has a nice low-keyed approach that is considerate, pleasant, and persistent. She immediately establishes common ground by linking her background to the receiver's experience. While seeking information and contacts, she clearly communicates her interest and enthusiasm by mentioning her educational background and travel experience. She invites the receiver to give her advice and thus creates the role of counselor for the receiver. She is not asking for a job—only information and advice. She'll most likely ask for referrals at the very end of this conversation. Best of all for a cold call, she sounds interesting, intelligent, and adventuresome. This is someone the receiver will probably decide to talk with for more than just a few minutes. Even though she is a stranger, he will probably like her and want to help her.

Referral With Gatekeeper

CALLER: *"Hi, this is Jim Taylor calling for Margaret Davis."*

RECEIVER: *"Miss Davis is in a meeting at present. Would you like to leave a message?"*

CALLER: *"Yes. Could you tell her Jim Taylor called. My number is 214-2790. Melissa Warner recommended that I call her about her work in . . . . I'll be in my office the rest of the day as well as between 9:00am and 4:00pm tomorrow. Thank you."*

ANALYSIS: Similar to the Terri Bays/Eric Walton cold call, the caller in this case immediately identifies himself and requests to speak with the person—the direct *"I'm X calling for Y"* approach. The gatekeeper will probably assume the caller knows the person. When the caller learns the person is not available, he leaves a message mentioning his referral contact. He has a high probability of getting a return call. He should leave the same message if he immediately encounters voice mail or the gatekeeper puts him through to a voice mailbox.

Referral Direct

CALLER: *"This is Terri Bays calling for Eric Walton."*

RECEIVER: *"Speaking."*

CALLER: *"John Pinkerton recommended that I call about your work in marketing."*

RECEIVER: *"How is John? I haven't spoken with him for some time."*

CALLER: *"John's doing great. He just returned from a two-month research project in the Ukraine. He's doing some fascinating work on a pilot agricultural marketing project sponsored by the UN. In fact, he recommended that I call you because you taught together in the Marketing Department at Michigan State University several years ago. He spoke very highly of you."*

RECEIVER: *"That's great to hear. John's always doing interesting and innovative work. Please give him my regards. So, how can I help you?"*

CALLER: *"I recently completed my Bachelor's degree in International Marketing at Indiana University. I speak Russian and have traveled extensively . . . "*

ANALYSIS: This is the most effective type of call you can make. It helps you quickly develop and expand your job search network. The caller already has a personal contact for establishing common ground. In contrast to other types of calls, referral calls often begin with a few moments of small talk. This type of small talk helps transfer the personal relationship existing between your referral and the receiver to you. It helps develop a cooperative relationship that should result in greater depth of information, advice, and referrals.

You need to make several types of follow-up calls throughout your job search. Failure to follow up is one of the major reasons many job seekers have difficulty making progress in the job market. You simply must follow up often and do so by telephone. The following are the most frequent type of follow-up calls you need to make.

Thank-You Follow-Up

CALLER: *"Hi, this is Jerry Winton calling for Jonathan Arthur."*

RECEIVER: *"Speaking."*

CALLER: *"Thanks so much for referring me to Jill Balinger last week. You were right. She really knows the leasing business, and I'm most impressed with the work she is doing in marine leasing. We had a wonderful talk this morning, and she invited me to meet with her next Tuesday about a position with her firm. I just wanted to let you know how much I appreciated your advice and reference. I'll let you know the outcome."*

ANALYSIS: Not only is such a thank-you call a thoughtful thing to do, it also may be a wise action at this time. Because Jerry called, Jonathan may next call his contact and put in a good word for Jerry's impending candidacy. After all, Jonathan was sufficiently impressed with Jerry to give him the referral to Jill in the first place. This thank-you call confirms Jonathan's wisdom for having referred Jerry to Jill. Similar types of thank-you calls are appropriate for other job search occasions, such as thanking someone for useful information and advice. Perhaps someone loaned you a book or counseled you about your job search. Make a thank-you follow-up call expressing your appreciation.

Resume or Application Follow-Up

CALLER: *"Hi, this is JoAnna Salem calling in reference to a letter and resume I sent to your office last week for the graphic design position you advertised in the Times. I wanted to check if you received it and if you had any questions."*

RECEIVER: *"Yes, we did get your resume. We're currently reviewing applications. I don't think we have any questions at this time. We'll give you a call if we do."*

CALLER: *"Do you know when you might be making the final decisions?"*

RECEIVER: *"We're trying to complete our review this week. We'll probably start interviewing sometime next week or the week* *after. I know Mr. Davis wants to get the position filled as soon as possible."*

CALLER: *"I'm really interested in the position. It's a perfect fit with my five years of experience in the publishing industry. Do let me know if you need any additional information. I would be happy to have you talk with several of my clients who know my work well."*

ANALYSIS: While this follow-up call yields some useful information about the decision-making process, it also may give your application added attention. The fact that the receiver had to check to see if they received your resume may help give your resume this attention. And it doesn't hurt to pitch yourself some more for the position. If you sound really good over the phone, the person may move you from the bottom of the pile to the top. You, in effect, conducted a screening interview for the position before being called by the employer for such an interview. This critical call may result in you being remembered more than other candidates. It's important that you not be too pushy when making such a call. You can easily turn off an employer by being too aggressive when making a follow-up call. You don't want to get remembered as a jerk! Get the information, make your point, and be remembered as a professional person who can communicate well with others.

Making Cold Calls For Uncovering Job Leads

Many people use the telephone to randomly uncover job leads. In fact, one approach of job clubs is to use the Yellow Pages to call employers directly to find out if they have vacancies. This type of call basically asks *"Do you have a job for me?"* It's the type of call that results in numerous rejections because (1) most employers contacted do not have vacancies at that particular moment and (2) employers are not keen about broadcasting vacancies to cold callers. Nonetheless, if you don't mind encountering numerous rejections and you are prepared to play the probability game, go ahead and try your luck. You might uncover two appropriate vacancies for every 100 cold calls you make. Your call might go something like this:

CALLER: *"Hi, this is Marcia Voris calling. Do you have any vacancies for word processors?"*

RECEIVER: *"Not at present."*

CALLER: *"Are you accepting applications?"*

RECEIVER: *"You can send us a resume if you wish. We'll keep it on file in case a vacancy would arise at another time. We do periodically hire for such positions."*

CALLER: *"To whom should I address my correspondence?"*

RECEIVER: *"Just send it to the Personnel Department."*

CALLER: *"I would really like to address it to a person."*

RECEIVER: *"It really doesn't matter, but go ahead and send it to Richard Merit who handles our resume database."*

CALLER: *"Thank you very much for your assistance. By the way, what is your name?"*

RECEIVER: *"Jeffrey Plant. I'm Mr. Merit's assistant."*

ANALYSIS: While we don't put much stock in making these types of cold calls, nonetheless, you can achieve some level of success if you move beyond just identifying vacancies. If you learn there are no vacancies at present, push on to find out about application procedures. Many organizations maintain resume banks which they refer to when vacancies arise. If the company accepts resumes or applications, try to get the name of the person you should contact. In this case, the caller was able to get the names of two people. When she submits her resume to Mr. Merit, she can mention in her letter how helpful Mr. Plant was and that he recommended that she submit her resume for consideration. She now has two contacts and a resume in this organization. Not bad for what was probably a two-minute call. If you make 100 such calls in a day, you should be able to collect 100 new names and submit 50 or more resumes.

Calling in Response to Ads and Vacancy Announcements

You also should network for information relevant to specific job vacancies. Most classified ads or vacancy announcements, for example, outline application procedures. Some may specifically state *"No phone calls please."* Nonetheless, the majority of employers will answer phone calls. Some may even encourage such calls because it indicates an interest in the position and company. At the same time, many applicants will call before they submit a resume and other documents for application. You are well advised to immediately call the company and ask for more information about the position. Read the ad carefully and list the questions you need addressed. You want to gather as much information about both the company and the position so you can "custom design" your resume and letter around the needs of the employer. Your call might go something like this:

CALLER:	*"Hi, this is Beverly Rodriguez calling. Your ad in today's Post for a dental assistant caught my attention. I'm thinking about applying, but I need more information. Could you tell me a little more about the position and The Cooper Group?"*
RECEIVER:	Responds to question with more information.
CALLER:	*"That sounds interesting. You must work for a very exciting organization. I'll definitely submit my application. To whom should I address my resume?"*
RECEIVER:	*"Send it to the attention of Tara Marks. She's in charge of handling this position."*
CALLER:	*"By the way, do you know when she expects to make the final decision?"*

ANALYSIS: By calling for more information about the position and organization, the caller may gain some useful "inside" information that will give him an advantage over the competition. For example, she might learn that it's a 30-hour a week position with no benefits. She might work with five doctors rather than one. The company may be seeking someone with at least five years of experience. The job might involve traveling to several nursing homes. She might learn about the salary range. In addition, she may get the name of the person handling the screening process and thus better personalize her correspondence. When it comes time to follow up, she has the name of the person to contact and knows the best time to call. Needless to say, this phone call may yield some very valuable information that will help you both screen the employer and better develop an employer-centered application.

Effective Telephone Closings

Similar to closing a job search letter, your telephone closing should end in some sort of future action. If you are closing a networking call, you should close with (1) an expression of gratitude, (2) a summary and interpretation of your conversation, and (3) a request for referrals. Your closing might go something like this:

CALLER: (EXPRESS GRATITUDE) *"I really appreciate the information you've given me on marketing opportunities in Eastern Europe and Russia.* (SUMMARIZE AND INTERPRET PREVIOUS CONVERSATION) *You've identified five pharmaceutical companies that seem to have established a strong presence in at least five of these countries. If I understand you correctly, you feel there may be some excellent opportunities with these companies for someone with my interests and skills. I'm especially encouraged by your observation that some of these companies do have entry-level marketing positions overseas.* (REQUEST FOR REFERRALS) *Could I ask one more favor? Do you know two or three other people in this field who would be willing to talk to me about such marketing opportunities?"*

RECEIVER: *"You're quite welcome. Let me think. Yes, why don't you give Mary Sellers at Vialoriate International a call. Her number is 281-0091. John Baird at Southern Pharmaceuticals also would be a good person to contact. His number is 281-1121. It's okay to use my name. I've known them for years. Really good people who know this area well. Tell them I recommended you call them."*

CALLER: *"Thanks so much. Please keep me in mind if you hear of any opportunities for someone with my interests. Would it be okay to send you a copy of my resume for your reference?"*

RECEIVER: *"Sure. I'd be happy to keep it on file and pass it along if I hear of any opportunities."*

CALLER: *"Thanks again. Goodbye."*

ANALYSIS: This is the perfect closing. The job seeker actually managed to turn the closing into two, hopefully three, important actions: (1) received two referrals, (2) got the receiver to accept and read a resume for reference, and (3) requested to be remembered for future referrals which may indeed turn into new job contacts. However, one word of caution. This closing is not complete until it is followed up with a thank you letter which includes a copy of the resume and a request for future referrals. The thank you letter should genuinely express your gratitude for the person's time and information. For examples of such thank you letters, see our *201 Dynamite Job Search Letters* (Impact Publications).

Answering Machine or Voice Mail Message

If you use an answering machine or voice mail system to manage your telephone calls, be sure you do so professionally. Nothing is more irritating than to waste people's time with a lengthy voice mail message. Nothing will kill your chances of getting a job quicker than to have an important caller hear an unprofessional or silly message on your answering machine. Keep your answering machine or voice mail message simple, professional, and to the point. This one works well:

"Sorry I missed your call. Please leave your name, telephone number, and a message at the sound of the beep. I'll return your call as soon as possible. Thanks for calling."

When networking by telephone, you can expect to encounter voice mail with at least 50 percent of your calls. More and more people in all types and sizes of organizations use voice mail to collect, screen, and retrieve their messages. When you make a phone call, expect to leave a message on voice mail rather than communicate directly with the individual you are calling. Many voice mail systems put you directly through to the individual's mail box whereas other systems may first route you through an operator or give you an operator option. If you have an operator option, ask the operator when you might best be able to contact the individual directly. He or she may be able to suggest a good time to call back. At the same time, leave a message in the individual's mail box.

Be sure to leave an informative message that is likely to result in a return call. People who use voice mail tend to be busy people who must screen which calls they will return. At least 30 percent of voice mail messages can be disregarded with little or no consequences. Many of these messages are cold calls intended to solicit business and acquire information. Make sure your message does not get screened into that 30 percent! Your message should state the following: (1) the purpose of your call, (2) the best time to contact you, and (3) your phone number. If you fail to clearly state your purpose, you may be screened out as a potential nuisance call. In your statement of purpose, try to connect yourself to the individual's interests. For example:

Referral Connection

"Jim Carlson suggested I call you about your work at ..."

Cold Call

"This is Janice Wilson at 717-234-1100. I'm calling in reference to your work in computer sales."

Expand your statement to include a complete message. A cold call message might include the following:

"Hi, this is Emily Zeiber. I'm calling about your innovative work in graphic design. It's now 1:45pm. I'll be in until 6:00pm today and all day tomorrow. My number is 221-4941. I look forward to speaking with you soon."

Use your own voice mail, an answering machine, an answering service, a beeper, or email if you are difficult to contact by phone. Looking for a job requires constant communication within an ever expanding network. Since you will be making numerous phone calls in developing your job search network, make sure you can be easily contacted. If someone returns your call and gets no answer or no opportunity to leave a message, don't expect that person to call you back again. Returning a call once is sufficient for most people who know little or nothing about you and the purpose of your call. At the very minimum you should use an answering machine or some form of voice mail. If you use the Internet or one of the commercial electronic communication systems, you may want to use your email address in your job search.

When leaving messages on voice mail, make sure your message motivates the receiver to return your call immediately. Most individuals prioritize which messages they will return. Your message should sufficiently grab the attention of the receiver to call you back immediately.

Your message should clearly state who you are and the nature of your call. Be clear and purposeful when leaving messages. Nothing is more irritating than to listen to a message that only includes a name and phone number. If people do not know who you are or why they should call you back, chances are they will screen out your call. They may assume you are trying to make a cold call to sell them something—calls they wish to avoid!

Your message should ask the receiver to take action—return your call as soon as possible. Again, leaving only a name and telephone number is an incomplete message. Since you want action, your message must call for action. You have two choices here. First, leave a message in which you ask the individual to call you back at such-and-such a time. Second, leave a message in which you indicate you plan to call back at such-and-such a time.

Try Approach Letters and Follow-Up Calls

You may want to use a more formal approach to gain access to referrals and new contacts. One strategy is to write an approach letter and follow it up with a phone call. Examples of approach letters are found on pages 91-94. These examples are aimed at two different audiences: personal contacts and strangers. The first two letters are written via personal contacts. In the last two examples—"cold turkey" letters—the writers are approaching individuals without prior contacts. In both cases the writers emphasize they are seeking information—not a job—and take the initiative to telephone the individual in order to make an appointment for an informational interview.

Approach Letter: Referral

821 Stevens Points
Boston, MA 01990

April 14, 20___

Terri Fulton
Director of Personnel
TRS Corporation
6311 W. Dover
Boston, MA 01991

Dear Ms. Fulton:

Alice O'Brien suggested that I contact you about my interest in personnel management. She said you are one of the best people to talk to in regard to careers in personnel.

I am leaving government after seven years of increasingly responsible experience in personnel. I am especially interested in working with a large private firm. However, before I venture further into the job market, I want to benefit from the experience and knowledge of others in the field who might advise me on opportunities for someone with my qualifications.

Perhaps we could meet briefly sometime during the next two weeks to discuss my career plans. I have several questions which I believe you could help clarify. I will call your office on Tuesday, April 22, to schedule a meeting time.

I look forward to learning from your experience.

Sincerely,

Katherine Kelly

Katherine Kelly

Approach Letter: Referral

1099 Seventh Avenue
Akron, OH 34522

December 10, 20___

Janet L. Cooper, Director
Architectural Design Office
RT Engineering Associates
621 West Grand Avenue
Akron, OH 34520

Dear Ms. Cooper:

John Sayres suggested that I write to you regarding my interest in
architectural drafting. He thought you would be a good person to give
me some career advice.

I am interested in an architectural drafting position with a firm which
specializes in commercial construction. As a trained draftsman, I have six
years of progressive experience in all facets of construction, from pouring
concrete to developing plans for $22 million in commercial and residential
construction. I am particularly interested in improving construction design
and building operations of shopping complexes.

Mr. Sayres mentioned you as one of the leading experts in this growing
field. Would it be possible for us to meet briefly? Over the next few months
I will be conducting a job search. I am certain your counsel would assist me
as I begin looking for new opportunities.

I will call your office next week to see if your schedule permits such a
meeting.

Sincerely,

John Albert

John Albert

Approach Letter: Cold Turkey

January 8, 20___

Sharon T. Avery
Vice President for Sales
Bentley Enterprises
529 W. Sheridan Road
Washington, DC 20011

Dear Ms. Avery:

I am writing to you because you know the importance of having a knowledgeable, highly motivated, and enthusiastic sales force to market your fine information processing equipment. I know because I have been impressed with your sales representative.

I am seeking your advice on how I might prepare for a career in your field. I have a sales and secretarial background—experience acquired while earning my way through college.

Within the coming months, I hope to begin a new career. My familiarity with word processing equipment, my sales experience, and my Bachelor's degree in communication have prepared me for the information processing field. I want to begin in sales and eventually move into a management level position.

As I begin my job search, I am trying to gather as much information and advice as possible before applying for positions. Could I take a few minutes of your time next week to discuss my career plans? Perhaps you could suggest how I can improve my resume—which I am now drafting—and who might be interested in my qualifications. I will call your office on Monday to see if such a meeting can be arranged.

I appreciate your consideration and look forward to meeting you.

Sincerely yours,

Gail S. Topper

Gail S. Topper

Approach Letter: Cold Turkey

August 29, 20___

Patricia Dotson, Director
Northeast Association for
   the Elderly
9930 Jefferson Street
New York, NY 10013

Dear Ms. Dotson:

I have been impressed with your work with the elderly. Your organization takes a community perspective in trying to integrate the concerns of the elderly with those of other community groups. Perhaps other organizations will soon follow your lead.

I am anxious to meet you and learn more about your work. My background with the city Volunteer Services Program involved frequent contact with elderly volunteers. From this experience I decided I preferred working primarily with the elderly.

However, before I pursue my interest further, I need to talk to people with experience in gerontology. In particular, I would like to know more about careers with the elderly as well as how my background might best be used in the field of gerontology.

I am hoping you can assist me in this matter. I would like to meet with you briefly to discuss several of my concerns. I will call next week to see if your schedule permits such a meeting.

I look forward to meeting you and learning from your experience.

Sincerely,

Carol Timms

Carol Timms

As we noted earlier, you should not enclose a copy of your resume with approach letters. The purpose of the letter is to make an appointment for an interview where you will seek job and career information, advice, and referrals. If you enclose a resume with this letter, you will probably send conflicting messages to your audience, that is, you want the person to find you a job.

Your **approach letter** should include the following elements:

Use Appropriate Openers

If you have a referral, tell the individual you are considering a career in _____. His or her name was given to you by ___ _____who suggested he or she might be a good person to give you useful information about careers in _____.

If you lack a referral to the individual and thus must use a "cold turkey" approach to making contact, you might begin your letter by stating that you are aware he or she has been at the forefront of _____ business—or whatever is both truthful and appropriate for the situation.

Make the Request

Demonstrate your thoughtfulness and courtesy rather than aggressiveness by mentioning that you know he or she is busy. You hope to schedule a mutually convenient time for a meeting to discuss your questions and career plans. Most people will be flattered by such a request and happy to talk with you about their work—if they have time and are interested in you.

Close It Right

In closing the letter, mention that you will call the person to see if an appointment can be arranged. Be specific by stating the time and day you will call—for example, *"Thursday at 2pm."* You must take the initiative in this manner and follow up the letter with a definite contact time. If you don't, you cannot expect to hear from the person. It is **your** responsibility to make the telephone call to schedule a meeting.

Be Careful About Enclosures

Do **not** enclose your resume with this approach letter. You should take your resume to the interview and present it as a topic of discussion near the end of your meeting. If you send it with the approach letter, you communicate a mixed and contradictory message. Remember your purpose for this interview: to gather information and advice. You are not—and never should be— asking for a job. A resume in a letter appears to be an application or a request for a job.

Most people will meet with you, assuming you are sincere. If the person tries to put you off when you telephone for an appointment, clearly state your purpose and emphasize that you are not looking for a job with this person—only requesting information and advice. If the person insists on putting you off, make the best of the situation: try to conduct the informational interview over the phone and request referrals. Follow up this conversation with a nice thank you letter in which you again state your intended purpose, mention your disap- pointment in not being able to meet and learn from this person, and ask to be remembered for future reference. You may enclose your resume with this letter.

Many individuals will want to conduct the informational interview over the telephone since he or she is too busy to see you. Such inter- views can yield just as good quality information and advice as face-to- face informational interviews. Welcome such interviews since they will save you a great deal of time. When you telephone the person, be prepared to conduct this interview over the phone. Have a list of ques- tions nearby that you planned to ask in the informational interview. Follow up this telephone interview in the same manner you would follow up any informational interview—with a thank-you letter. You should also enclose your resume with this letter in which you ask to be remembered and referred to others.

Whether you conduct the informational interview in person or over the telephone, treat this interview as an important screening interview. While you are ostensibly seeking information and advice, informational interviews can quickly turn into job interviews should you by chance contact an individual who also has a vacancy or who may create a new position around your qualifications. Therefore, you need to be at your best. Be sure you communicate your competence, intelligence, honesty, and likability in this interview. These are the same qualities you should communicate in a formal job interview.

Prepare Your Questions

In the informational interview **you** are the interviewer. It is you who is primarily seeking information. Therefore, you need to think through, prior to the interview, several questions you want to probe. For example, you should ask several of these questions:

"What type of skills and knowledge does one need to perform this job?"

"What are some of the particular advantages and disadvantages of this type of work?"

"What type of advancement opportunities are there?"

"What is the future outlook like in this line of work?"

"Could you describe a typical work day for me?"

"What do you like about your work?"

"What do you dislike about your work?"

"What are the normal salary ranges for entry into this type of work?"

"How would I best acquire the necessary skills to perform this job?"

"What type of objections might employers have to my background?"

"What might be the best way to approach prospective employers?"

"How did you go about finding this job?"

Your initial questions should focus on how to improve your job search rather than gather information on the person's company. If, as the interview progresses, it seems appropriate to ask specific questions about the company, go ahead and ask, but be careful. Remember, you are not interviewing for a position with this company—**you are seeking information about a job or career in a given field**. You do not want to wear out your welcome by making the individual feel uncomfortable with questions about a job vacancy this person might have for you. And people do get uncomfortable when you start asking for a job!

Conduct the Interview Well

If you approach people in the right manner, at least 50 percent of those you contact for informational interviews will meet with you. Some job hunters are never refused such an interview. Assuming you, too, are successful in scheduling these interviews, what do you do at the interview?

In the informational interview you want to focus your questions around four outcomes that literally define an effective informational interview:

- Information
- Advice
- Referrals
- To be remembered

At the same time, you are trying to impress upon the people you are interviewing that you possess the essential ingredients for being an outstanding employee: competent, intelligent, honest, enthusiastic, spontaneous, and likable. These are the types of people individuals like to refer to others as well as hire for their own organization.

> *The interview should take no more than 45 minutes.*

While the informational interview is relatively unstructured, it should follow a general pattern of questions and answers. The interview should take no more than 45 minutes. However, it may go much longer if your interviewee gets carried away in sharing his or her experiences and giving you advice. Some interviews may go on for two or more hours. But plan to cover your questions in a 30- to 45-minute period.

For best results, the interview should go something like this. The interview will begin with a few minutes of small talk—the weather, traffic, mutual acquaintances, a humorous observation. Next, you should initiate the interview by emphasizing your appreciation:

> *"Thank you again for taking time to see me today. I appreciate your willingness to speak with me about my career plans. It is a subject which is very important to me at this juncture of my life."*

Follow this statement with a re-statement of your purpose, as you mentioned in your letter and/or over the telephone:

> *"I am in the process of exploring several job and career alternatives. I know what I do well and enjoy doing. But before I make any decisions, I am trying to benefit from the counsel of individuals, such as you, who have a great deal of experience in the area of __*
> *_____. I am particularly interested in learning more about opportunities, necessary skills, responsibilities, advantages, disadvantages, and the future outlook for this field."*

Such a general statement should elicit a response from the individual. It should put him or her at ease by stressing your need at this time for information and counsel rather than a job.

Be sure you communicate your purpose at this stage and that you know what you want to do. If you don't, the individual may feel you are wasting his or her time. Thus, you need to know your strengths as well as have a clearly defined objective **prior to** this interview.

> *Be sure you communicate your purpose and that you know what you want to do.*

The next section of the interview should focus on several *"how"* and *"what"* questions concerning specific jobs or careers:

- Duties and responsibilities

- Knowledge, skills, abilities, and qualifications

- Work environments—fellow employees, deadlines, stress, problems

- Advantages and disadvantages

- Future outlook

- Salary ranges

Each of these questions can take a great deal of time to answer and discuss. Therefore, prioritize the ones you most need to ask, and try to keep the conversation moving on the various subjects.

Your second major line of questioning should center on your job search. Here you want to solicit useful advice for improving your job search. In relation to the previous job-content questions, you now want to know how to:

- Acquire the required skills

- Find a job related to this field

- Overcome employers' objections to you

- Identify both advertised and unadvertised job vacancies

- Develop new job leads

- Approach prospective employers

Your last major set of questions should deal with your resume. Remember, you have taken copies of your resume to this interview but the person has not seen your resume yet. You have done this purposefully so the individual will get to know you prior to seeing your paper qualifications. At this point you ask the person to critique your resume. Give him or her a copy and ask these questions:

"Is this an appropriate type of resume for the jobs I have outlined?"

"If an employer received this resume in the mail, how do you think he or she would react to it?"

"What do you see as possible weaknesses or areas that need to be improved?"

"What about the length, paper quality and color, layout, and typing? Are they appropriate?"

"How might I best improve the form and content of the resume?"

By doing this, the interviewee will be forced to read your resume—which is a good summary of what you talked about earlier in the interview. Most important of all, he or she will give you useful advice on how to improve and target your resume.

Your last two questions are actually requests to be **referred and remembered**. As you express your gratitude for the person's time, ask for referrals:

> *"Thanks so much for all your assistance. I have learned a great deal today. Your advice will certainly help me give my job search better direction. I would like to ask one more favor if I could. By conducting research on various jobs, I am trying to benefit from the counsel of several people. Do you know two or three other people who might be willing to meet with me, as you have today?"*

Just before you leave, ask to be **remembered** for future reference:

> *"While I know you may not know of a job opening at present for someone with my qualifications, I would appreciate it if you could keep me in mind if you learn of any openings. Please feel free to pass my name on to anyone you feel might be interested in my qualifications."*

Make sure you leave a copy of your resume with this person so that he or she has something tangible to refer and remember you by.

The examples of dialogues throughout this book are presented to show how one might conduct a phone or face-to-face interview. Certainly you should formulate your strategy in advance of a meeting or phone call. However, under no circumstances should you write out and memorize word-for-word what you plan to say. It will sound memorized and you may even forget and stumble through it. Consider your goals—what you need to convey and what you need to find out—formulate a general plan, make brief notes if you need to, but your conversation should be spontaneous, natural, and enthusiastic.

Let's examine another example of an informational interview as we put all these elements together:

Informational Interview Dialogue

INTRODUCTION: *"Good morning, Mr. Taylor. It's a pleasure to meet you. I really appreciate your taking time to see me and answer some questions that are important to my future."*

PURPOSE AND EXPECTATIONS: *"As I mentioned in my letter, I am exploring different job and career opportunities. The type of work you do interests me very much. I want to learn more about _____ (technical writing, sales, personnel administration). Let me emphasize again that I don't expect you to have or even know of a job vacancy."*

JOB REQUIREMENTS, RELATIONSHIPS, ENVIRONMENT: *"If it's okay with you, I'd like to ask you some questions about this type of work":*

- *"What are some of the regular tasks and activities involved in (occupation)?"*

- *"What skills and abilities are required to do a good job?"*

- *"What kinds of relationships with others are expected or necessary in performing the job?"*

- *"What is the work environment like in terms of pressure, deadlines, routines, new activities?"*

NOTE: The discussion of work requirements should take 15-20 minutes.

TRANSITION: *"This has been very helpful. You've given me information I've not read nor even considered before."*

OCCUPATIONAL OUTLOOK AND APPLICATION ADVICE: *"I'd like to shift the focus a bit and ask your opinion about the future employment outlook in the field of (occupation)":*

- *"Are job prospects good, stable, or very competitive?"*

- *"What local organizations employ people in (occupation)?"*

- *"What's the best way to apply for jobs in (occupation)?"*

- *"What is the range for entry-level (or whatever is appropriate) salaries for this type of job?"*

NOTE: Discussion of employment outlook, job hunting, and application procedures should take approximately 10 minutes.

RESUME EVALUATION: *"If you don't mind, could you look at my resume? Perhaps you could comment on its clarity or make suggestions for improving it?"*

- *"Is this resume appropriate for the jobs I've outlined?"*

- *"How do you think an employer would respond to this resume?"*

- *"Do you have any suggestions on how I might strengthen it?"*

NOTE: These questions will force the individual to read your resume and keep a copy for reference and referrals.

OCCUPATIONAL OPPORTUNITIES FOR YOU: *"How would someone with my background get started in (occupation)? What kinds of positions could I qualify for?"*

- *"You've been most generous with your time, and the information you've given me is most useful. It clarifies and reinforces a number of points for me. I have two final requests":*

"The jobs you thought might be appropriate for someone with my skills sound interesting, and I'd like to find out more about those possibilities. Do you know individuals in those kinds of jobs who would be willing—like yourself—to provide me with additional information?"

NOTE: About half will provide you with multiple referrals.

"Finally, I would appreciate it if you could keep my resume for reference in case you hear of a vacancy appropriate for someone with my background and interests. Please feel free to pass my name on to others who might be interested in my interests and qualifications."

EXPRESS   *"Thanks again for taking the time to see me.*
GRATITUDE: *You've been very helpful and I appreciate it."*

After completing this interview, you should send a nice **thank-you letter** to this person. Not only is this a thoughtful thing to do, it is also a wise thing to do if you wish to be remembered and referred. Genuinely express your gratitude for the person's time and help, and reiterate your wish to be remembered and referred. Page 105 includes an example of such a post-informational interview thank-you letter.

Provide Useful and Quality Information

You will often get more honest information in an informational interview than in a job interview. In trying to fill vacancies, employers cannot be objective because they also are attempting to sell you on the benefits of working for them. Informational interviews tend to be less persuasive.

Informational interviews will help you determine if you are interested in a particular career field or job. For example, in our work with college students, we encounter many who aspire to become attorneys. However, a typical conception is based on seeing too many episodes of *L.A. Law* and *Perry Mason*. The image of legal work often is one of standing before the jury dramatically arguing a case. Once these students realize that the two most important skills attorneys use

Thank-You Letter

9910 Thompson Drive
Cleveland, OH 43382

June 21, 20___

Jane Evans, Director
Evans Finance Corporation
2122 Forman Street
Cleveland, OH 43380

Dear Ms. Evans:

Your advice was most helpful in clarifying my questions on careers in finance. I am now reworking my resume and have included many of your thoughtful suggestions. I will send you a copy next week.

Thanks so much for taking time from your busy schedule to see me. I will keep in contact and follow through on your suggestion to see Sarah Cook about opportunities with the Cleveland-Akron Finance Company.

Sincerely,

Daryl Haines

Daryl Haines

are research and counseling, many quickly lose interest in this career field.

Conducting informational interviews can help you avoid jobs or careers that are not right for you. Whether you are looking forward to a job after you finish school or are already in the workforce but desire to make a job or career change, informational interviews are valuable tools.

Expect Serendipity

When conducting informational interviews, you may occasionally uncover a job opening with the person you are interviewing. Sometimes the company may consider creating a position for you because they are so impressed with your credentials. We have seen this happen with individuals we have counseled. But these are exceptions rather than the rule. Do not go into an informational interview expecting to come out with anything more than information, advice, referrals, and the promise to be remembered.

Follow Principles of Successful Networking

As you conduct informational interviews and network with many individuals, keep these seven rules in mind:

1. Look for a job that is fit for you rather than try to fit yourself into an available position.

2. Target your job search toward specific positions, organizations, and individuals. Most shotgun approaches tend to be ineffective.

3. Conduct a persistent prospecting campaign to continually expand your network and replenish contacts that lead to more contacts and informational interviews.

4. Increase your number of acceptances by conducting many informational interviews. When you ask for information, advice, and referrals, few people will turn you down. Most people you ask will be flattered and eager to assist you.

5. If your job search bogs down, chances are you need to substantially increase your daily prospecting activities as well as the number of informational interviews you conduct each week. Persistence, based on an understanding of probability, pays off in the long run.

6. Always send a thank-you letter to those who take the time to talk with you. Thoughtful people tend to be remembered people.

7. In the end, your job search success is a direct function of how well you network according to the principles of prospecting and informational interviewing.

If you follow these simple rules, your networking activities are most likely to turn into actual interviews which lead to offers for high quality jobs.

If you decide not to engage in networking and informational interviews, all is not lost. Each year millions of people do get interviews and job offers by passively submitting applications and resumes in response to vacancy announcements. If you don't network, be prepared to spend a great deal of time on the inherently frustrating advertised job market where you are likely to experience high competition and numerous rejections. Compared to individuals who regularly network for information, advice, and referrals, you'll spend twice as much time looking for a job. And the jobs you find in the advertised job market may not be of the quality you aspire to.

If you want to shorten your job search time, find quality jobs, and target jobs that best fit your particular mix of interests and skills, try networking for information, advice, and referrals.

6

Maintain and Expand Your Network

NETWORKING IS NOT SOMETHING YOU SHOULD turn on and off, depending on whether you are looking for a job. Networking should become an ongoing process both during and after your job search. It should play an important role in advancing your career within and among organizations. But it can only continue playing a role if you pay particular attention to the details of maintaining and expanding your network.

Remember Follow-Up and Feedback

Effective networkers know the importance of follow-up and feedback both during the job search and once they accept a job offer. They recognize that follow-up and feedback are essential ingredients in the process of maintaining and further expanding their networks.

When you receive a referral from one of your networking contacts, be sure to follow up the referral with a telephone call. Chances are your contact has already talked to the referral and informed him or her about your interests and indicated that you would contact them soon. Both individuals are expecting you to call. If you fail to follow up on referral efforts, your contacts may quickly dismiss you as someone who is wasting their time and who is also inconsiderate.

When you receive a referral, you should do two things:

- Contact the referral by telephone to arrange a meeting or conduct the informational interview over the phone. Mention in your opening statement that *"Mr. X suggested that I contact you concerning my interest in careers in _____."* In many, but not all, cases your contact will have called this person ahead of time to inform him of your impending call.

- After conducting an informational interview with a referral, thank the referral source. You need to do this in order to emphasize the fact that you indeed did follow up on the referral and to reemphasize your continuing interest in additional referrals. This is also a good time to provide your contact with feedback on your job search progress. Individuals like to know if their personal efforts produce results. They will remember you for giving them this feedback.

Throughout your job search you will be collecting names, addresses, and phone numbers of individuals who are the subjects of your prospecting, networking, and informational interviewing activities. Once you accept a job offer, be sure to contact individuals in your network who assisted you with information, advice, and referrals. Send them a thoughtful letter in which you (1) inform them of your new position and (2) thank them

> ***Be sure to follow up the referral with a telephone call.***

for their assistance. Individuals who played the most important role in your job search should also receive a phone call from you in which you again inform them of your new position and express your gratitude for their assistance. Sending flowers or a small gift to the most important individuals leaves a lasting positive impression.

Doing follow-up and providing feedback to members of your network is not only a thoughtful thing to do; it is also a wise thing to do. It results in one other important outcome for maintaining and expanding your network in the future: you will most likely be **remembered for future reference**. And this is exactly what you want to do since your new position may be only one of several new positions you acquire during your career. Within another three to five years you may decide it is time to conduct another job search. When that happens, you should have in place a well developed network of individuals who are willing and able to assist you with your job search. If you fail to provide members of your present network with follow-up and feedback, they are less likely to assist you in the future.

Network On the Job

Networking should become a part of your daily routines both on and off the job. Once you begin your new job, remember that your organization is made up of many people who can be helpful in advancing your career within the organization. You should quickly analyze the organizational environment. Learn who has power and influence, whom you should avoid, and who might make a useful mentor, advisor, or friend.

If you want to get ahead on the job, you should run with winners—those who have influence and power to get ahead. Therefore, you will want to continue your prospecting, networking, and informational interviewing activities on the job. However, you must refocus these activities on the career advancement process. What, for example, are the major criteria for getting ahead in this organization? How important is "whom you associate with" to advancing in this organization? Are you associating with the right people and are you clearly communicating your competence, honesty, trustworthiness, enthusiasm, and likability to these individuals? Perhaps more important, are the so-called winners —those you need to run with in order to get ahead—worth the time and effort? You may decide career advancement via such individuals is less than preferable to working elsewhere in the future. The phenomenon of "working for a jerk" is more widespread than many employees have been willing to admit!

Remember, whether we like it or not, all organizations are more or less political in terms of their internal relationships. The sooner you learn about the interpersonal structure of your organization, the sooner you can begin networking with the right people.

Develop Linkages to Other Organizations

Regardless of how happy you may be with your present job, there may come a time when you decide to move on to other opportunities in other organizations. You may decide you have advanced as far as possible in

Organization X; it's time to look for greener pastures where you can better use your talents. Or you may wish to change careers after deciding you would like to do something else with your life. On a more negative side, you may find yourself on the "outs" with your present employer, experience termination, or are just plain unhappy with your present job. Whatever the rationale for looking outside your present organization, there is a 90 percent probability that you will change jobs and careers again within the next 10 years.

If you are like many other people, you suddenly turn off the job search once you find employment. You are no longer concerned with setting career goals, conducting research on organizations, writing resumes, networking, and interviewing. It's only when you are forced to look for a job that you again activate the job search process. When this happens, job seekers find it difficult to get "back into" the job market because their job search skills—especially resume writing and networking—have become so rusty.

Networking should be the one job search skill you keep active while you are employed. Assuming you will one day be looking for another job outside your present organization, it is a good idea to develop, maintain, and expand your networks with professionals in similar types of positions and organizations. You can do this by joining professional organizations. But more important, you should become active in these organizations. For example, many of the associations listed in Chapter 7 are organized at the national and local levels. Local chapters meet regularly to promote their professional interests. They function as networks for exchanging information, advice, and referrals. Many also conduct networking activities and operate job search and placement services for their members.

Transcend the Job By Being in Demand

Have you ever wanted to be in the enviable position of having employers knock on your door rather than you having to always knock on their doors? You can achieve a turnaround in the job finding process through your networking activities.

At some point in your career you may be able to transcend the job search process altogether. You do this by achieving a level of recognition that results in other people contacting you with job opportunities. If you can be regularly remembered and referred, you may never need to look for another job because the jobs will come looking for you.

Through your regular networking activities, you've come to know numerous individuals who remember your interests, skills, and accomplishments. You've developed mutually supportive professional relations with most people in your immediate and extended network. While your initial networking activities were aimed at expanding the number of people you know, your long-term networking activities result in changing the direction of networking benefits. You'll shift the rules of the hiring game from *"whom you know"* to *"who knows you."* Employers or their representatives—headhunters, executive search firms, and other intermediaries—will knock on your door with questions such as *"Are you interested in making a job change?"* *"What's your situation with your present employer?"* *"Are you planning to make any career moves within the foreseeable future?"*

Whatever your professional background or interest, you should join organizations that provide such networking experiences. Active members are those who are also remembered by fellow members. Some are remembered so well that they are often approached by fellow members with new job opportunities. This is the ultimate result of excellent networking: you no longer need to look for a job; you've placed yourself in a position whereby you are in demand by employers. Using their own networking activities, employers, headhunters, and executive search firms come to you with job offers. They try to persuade you to leave your present job to join their organization. Indeed, if you network well, you may never have to look for another job and engage in a time consuming and often frustrating job search process; instead, the jobs will come looking for you!

> **If you network, you may never need to look for another job because the jobs will come looking for you.**

If and when you decide to make a job or career move, fellow members of your association will most likely play a central role in your job search. They will assist you with information, advice, and referrals that should lead to job interviews and offers. In this sense, your next job search should be much easier to conduct than your present one. Your networks will be in place; you merely need to "spread the word" that you are looking for other opportunities. Members of your network should be willing and able to provide you with job leads that will turn into new and exciting opportunities.

7

Networks For Networking

ALTHOUGH NETWORKING TAKES PLACE AMONG individuals, formal organizations provide the settings for many networking activities. When looking for employment, you should target your networking toward those organizations that offer job opportunities. When working within an organization, many of your networking activities will take place among co-workers, supervisors, and other influential people within the organization. At the same time, you should maintain linkages with individuals in organizations outside your employer's company. These organizations may consist of professional and trade associations, companies performing similar or competing functions, or community and social groups. All of these organizations are potential sources for your networking activities.

Professional and Trade Associations

Professional and trade associations function as some of the most important networks for finding jobs and advancing careers. These associations operate both inside and outside organizations. Some associations, such as the AFL-CIO, are primarily oriented toward promoting the employment interests of workers by focusing on wages and benefits. Other associations, such as the National Association of

Manufacturers (NAM), are organized to promote the interests of employers and their companies. All of these organizations provide services to their dues-paying members. These include anything from a monthly magazine, newsletter, and website to insurance, travel, training, and job placement benefits. Indeed, many such associations maintain job bank and referral services, periodically sponsor networking meetings, and provide job search training for their members.

Most important for anyone seeking employment and advancing careers, professional and trade associations link individuals who work for one employer with individuals who work for other employers. In so doing, they provide a critical communication and networking **bridge** between organizations that assist members in making job and career moves from one organization to another.

Networking Communities

Several gender, age, ethnic, community, and occupational groups of individuals are more highly networked than others because of their high degree of organizational activity. Women, the military, executives, high-tech, and several minority groups, for example, sponsor their own associations where they often focus on networking activities relating to their career. Some, such as Forty Plus (*www.fortyplus.org*) and the Five O'Clock Club (*www.fiveoclockclub.org*), solely function as job networking groups. Others, such as the DC Web Women (*www.dcweb women.org*), are multipurpose networks for exchanging ideas, providing technical support, advancing careers, and changing jobs.

Take, for example, another case of the Washington, DC metropolitan area. This is a smart high-income community that has one of the most enviable high-tech job markets in the world, because of its role as the center of the Internet universe (over 60 percent of the world's Internet traffic flows through this area). High-tech industries continue to rapidly expand, especially along the Dulles Corridor around Reston and Herndon, Virginia—Washington, DC's equivalent to California's Silicon Valley. This is a metro area where the demand for high-tech workers far outstrips the supply of qualified candidates and where many young "techies" would like to become instant Internet millionaires after sleeping under their desks for several months! At the same time, Washingtonians have always been savvy networkers (see pages 25-27), whether they work for government, nonprofit organizations, law firms, educational institutions, government contractors, corporations, or the media. Accordingly, the high-tech community is well organized with numerous professional associations and membership groups which also function as key networking groups for changing jobs and advancing careers. Anyone in the high-tech sector in the Washington, DC metro area will belong to some of these organizations and use them for networking purposes:

Association for Information Technology Professionals:	*www.aitp.org*
Association For Interactive Media:	*www.interactivehq.org*
Association of Internet Professionals (DC):	*www.dcaip.org*
Association of Women in Computing – National Capital Chapter:	*www.awcncc.org*
DC Web Women:	*www.dcwebwomen.org*
Dingman Center for Entrepreneurship:	*www.mbs.umd.edu/dingman*
Electronic Industries Alliance:	*www.eia.org*
Fairfax County Chamber of Commerce:	*www.fccc.org*
Greater Washington Society of Association Executives:	*www.gwsae.org*
High Technology Council of Maryland:	*www.mdhitech.org*
Internet Society:	*www.dcisoc.org*
Information Technology Association of America:	*www.itaa.org*
Information Technology Resellers Association:	*info@itra.net*
Netpreneur.org (Morino Institute):	*www.netpreneur.org*
Northern Virginia Technology Council (NVTC):	*www.nvtc.org*
Software & Information Industry Association (SIIA):	*www.siia.net*
The Information Management Exchange (TIME):	*www.timeus.org*
The New Media Society of Washington:	*www.newmediasociety.org*
Virginia Center for Innovative Technology:	*www.cit.org*
Washington D.C. Technology Council:	*www.wdctech.net*
Women in Technology:	*www.womenintechnology.org*

Specialized computer programmers also have their own set of organizations for networking:

Capital Area SQL Server	
User's Group:	*www.ntpro.org/sql/index.html*
Capital PC User Group:	*http://cpcug.org*
D.C. Area Sybase User's Group:	*www2.dgsys.com/~dcasug*
E-Commerce and Intranet	
Applications Group:	*www.ntpro.org/ecommerce index.asp*
Northern Virginia Linux	
Users Group:	*http://novalug.tux.org*
NT Server User Group of Virginia:	*www.ntpro.org/netserver*
Washington Apple Pi:	*www.wap.org/info*
Washington Area Computer	
User Group (WAC):	*www.tiac.net/users/wacug*
Washington Area Informix	
Users Group (WAIUG):	*www.iiug.org/~waiug*
Washington Area SGML/XML	
Users Group:	*www.eccnet.com/sgmlug*
Washington D.C. Area Linux	
User Group (DCLUG):	*http://wauug.erols.com/dclinux*
Washington D.C. Area	
Perl Mongers:	*http://dc.pm.org*

Much of this association-based networking is further extended into other forums for networking. The Revolution Lounge in Herndon, Virginia, for example, regularly functions as a recruitment center (free booze and hors d'oeuvres) for dot-com companies in search of Internet talent; individuals on HireStrategy.com's mailing list get regular updates of upcoming "networking/recruiting events" at this high-tech bar (no jackets and ties nor speeches for this beer and wine drinking digital generation of job seekers).

Deliberately organized as networking groups, many of these associations and groups meet on a monthly basis. They usually host formal face-to-face meetings, informal seminars, discussions, special events, breakfasts, luncheons, and other networking opportunities where participants have an opportunity to meet new people, engage in small talk, drop names, talk about achievements, and exchange ideas, business cards, and resumes. They further extend their networking activities into 24/7 cyberspace through active websites, which include chat groups, job postings, employer profiles, and resume databases. Email functions as the lifeblood for keeping these networks vibrant.

Information Sources

You will discover thousands of organizations and associations that perform linkage functions, as well as provide networking opportunities, relevant to finding jobs and advancing careers. Most of these organizations can be easily accessed by surveying a few key directories that provide the names, addresses, telephone/fax numbers, and websites of— as well as inside information on—these organizations. The two most important directories are:

> *National Trade and Professional Associations* (Washington, DC: Columbia Books, annual)

> *Encyclopedia of Associations* (Detroit, MI: Thompson Learning, annual)

While more than 135,000 associations function within the United States, these two directories provide information on more than 25,000 of the most important trade and professional associations. The directories are found in many libraries or they can be ordered directly from Impact Publications.

You'll also find directories of associations online. Begin by exploring these useful sites:

Associations on the Net:	*www.ipl.org/ref/AON*
AssociationCentral.com:	*www.associationcentral.com*
American Society of Association Executives:	*www.assaenet.org*

Key Associations

The following list of organizations is only a sampling of the many thousands of professional and trade associations you will discover as you conduct research on these centers for networking. We include three examples for each category. The categories are organized according to different occupational groups. As you conduct further research, you will discover that engineers, health care workers, insurance professionals,

and numerous other occupations have many different associations repre-
senting different types of professionals and industries. For example, you
will find more than 100 associations for engineers. These associations
specialize according to the type of engineering: cost, chemical, mining,
petroleum, civil, gas, naval, mechanical, safety, energy, audio, biome-
dical, insulated cable, ceramic, packaging, logistic, automotive, broad-
cast, flight test, explosives, and the list goes on and on. Therefore, you
need to specify the type of association appropriate for your particular
skills and interests. You can only do this by spending some time
researching the various types of trade and professional associations.

While our addresses and telephone numbers relate to the national
headquarters, most of these associations also are organized at the state
and local levels. Very large associations may, for example, have local
chapters centered in major cities and regions. These chapters may
operate separate websites, publish their own newsletters, meet on a
monthly basis, sponsor networking events, and provide job search and
placement services to their members. These community-based groups
may become your most valuable networking resource.

It would be to your benefit to identify two or more associations
relevant to your professional interests. Contact the headquarters office
for information on services and membership. If the association has a
local chapter, contact a few of the members to find out more about the
association. You may be pleasantly surprised to find a group of professionals sharing your interests. If you decide to join, we urge you to
get involved by becoming a **participant** in the organization rather than
just a dues-paying spectator. Networking via such associations works
best when you become noticed by other members because of your
participation and involvement in furthering the goals of the organization
and thus its members.

The Organizations

Accounting

American Accounting Association: 5717 Bessie Drive, Sarasota, FL
34223-2399, Tel. 941/921-7747. Website: *http://aaa-edu.org*

Institute of Management Accountants: 10 Paragon Drive, Montvale,
NJ 07645-1760, Tel. 201/573-9000. Website: *www.imanet.org*

National Society of Accountants: 1010 North Fairfax St., Alexandria, VA 22314-1574, Tel. 703/549-6400. Website: *www.nsacct.org*

Advertising

American Advertising Federation: 1101 Vermont Ave., NW, Suite 500, Washington, DC 20005-6306, Tel. 202/898-0089. Website: *www.aaf.org*

American Association of Advertising Agencies: Chrysler Building, 405 Lexington Avenue, 18th Floor, New York, NY 10174-1801, Tel. 212/682-2500. Website: *www.aaaa.org*

Association of National Advertisers: 708 Third Avenue, 33rd Floor, New York, NY 10017, Tel. 212/697-5950. Website: *www.ana.net*

Banking and Finance

American Bankers Association: 1120 Connecticut Ave., NW, Washington, DC 20036, Tel. 202/663-5382. Website: *www.aba.com*

American Financial Services Association: 919 18th Street, NW, 3rd Floor, Washington, DC 20006, Tel. 202/296-5544. Website: *www.american.finsvcs.org*

National Bankers Association: 1513 P Street, NW, Washington, DC 20005, Tel. 202/588-5432. Website: *www.nationalbanks.org*

Business

Alpha Kappa Psi: 9595 Angola Court, Indianapolis, IN 46268-1119, Tel. 317/872-1553. Website: *www.akpsi.com*

Chamber of Commerce of the United States of America: 1615 H St., NW, Washington, DC 20062-2000, Tel. 202/659-6000. Website: *www.uschamber.org*

National Business Association: 5151 Beltline Road, Suite 1150, Dallas, TX 75240-6739, Tel. 972/458-0900. Website: *www.national business.org*

Chemical Industry

American Chemical Society: 1155 16th St., NW, Washington, DC 20036, Tel. 202/872-4600. Website: *www.acs.org*

Chemical Manufacturers Association: 1300 Wilson Blvd., Arlington, VA 22209-2307, Tel. 703/741-5000. Website: *www.cmahq.com*

PACE: Paper, Allied-Industrial, Chemical and Energy Workers International Union: 3340 Perimeter Hill Drive, Nashville TN 37211, Tel. 615-834-8590. Website: *www.paceunion.org*

Communications

Association For Business Communications: 17 Lexington Avenue, New York, NY 10010, Tel. 212-387-1620. Website: *www.theabc.org*

Communications Marketing Association: 1201 Mt. Kemble, Morristown, NJ 07960, Tel. 973/425-1700. Website: *www.cma.org*

International Communication Association: 3530 Forest Lane, Suite 200, Dallas, TX 75234, Tel. 972/620-7020. Website: *www.ICAnet.com*

Counseling

American Counseling Association: 5999 Stevenson Ave., Alexandria, VA 22304-3300, Tel. 703/823-9800. Website: *www.counseling.org*

National Board For Certified Counselors, Inc.: 3 Terrace Way, Suite D, Greensboro, NC 27403-3660, Tel. 336/547-0607. Website: *www. nbcc.org*

National Rehabilitation Counseling Association: 8807 Sudley Rd., Suite 102, Manassas, VA 22110-4719, Tel. 703/361-2077. Website: *www.nrca-net.org*

Economics

American Economic Association: 2014 Broadway, Suite 305, Nashville, TN 37203-2418, Tel. 615/322-2595. Website: *www.vanderbilt. edu/AEA*

Econometric Society: Department of Economics, Northwestern University, Evanston, IL 60208-2600, Tel. 847/491-3615. Website: *www. econometricsociety.org*

National Association of Business Economists: 1233 20th St., NW, Suite 505, Washington, DC 20036-2304, Tel. 202/463-6223. Website: *www.nabe.com*

Education

American Association For Higher Education: One Dupont Circle, NW, Suite 360, Washington, DC 20036-1110, Tel. 202/293-6440. Website: *www.aahe.org*

American Federation of Teachers: 555 New Jersey Avenue, NW, Washington, DC 20001, Tel. 202/879-4400. Website: *www.aft.org*

National Education Association: 1201 16th St., NW, Washington, DC 20036-3290, Tel. 202/833-4000. Website: *www.nea.org*

Electricity and Electronics

American Electronics Association: 5201 Great American Parkway, Suite 520, Santa Clara, CA 95054, Tel. 408/987-4200. Website: *www. aeanet.org*

Electronic Industries Association: 2500 Wilson Blvd., Arlington, VA 22201, Tel. 703/907-7500. Website: *www.eia.org*

Semiconductor Industry Association: 181 Metro Drive, Suite 450, San Jose, CA 95110, Tel. 408/436-6600. Website: *www.semichips.org*

Engineering

American Society For Engineering Management: P.O. Box 820, Rolla, MO 65402, Tel. 573/341-2101. Website: *www.emba.uvm.edu/~asem*

Association of Energy Engineers: 4025 Pleasantdale Rd., Suite 420, Atlanta, GA 30340, Tel. 404/447-5083. Website: *www.aeecenter.org*

National Society of Professional Engineers: 1420 King St., Alexandria, VA 22314-2794, Tel. 703/684-2800. Website: *www.nspe.org*

Government

American Federation of Government Employees: 80 F St., NW, Washington, DC 20001, Tel. 202/639-6419. Website: *www.afge.org*

American Federation of State, County, and Municipal Employers: 1625 L St., NW, Washington, DC 20036, Tel. 202/452-4800. Website: *www.afscme.org*

American Society for Public Administration: 1120 G St., NW, Suite 700, Washington, DC 20005-3885, Tel. 202/393-7878. Website: *www.aspanet.org*

Health Care and Medicine

American Health Planning Association: 7245 Arlington Blvd., Suite 300, Falls Church, VA 22042, Tel. 703/573-3103. Website: *www.apha net.org*

American Medical Association: 515 N. State St., Chicago, IL 60610, Tel. 312/464-5000. Website: *www.ama-assn.org*

National Association of Public Hospitals and Health Systems: 1301 Pennsylvania Ave., Suite 950, Washington, DC 20004, Tel. 202/585-0100. Website: *www.naph.org*

Information Science and Technology

American Society For Information Science: 8720 Georgia Ave., Suite 501, Silver Spring, MD 20910-3602, Tel. 301/495-0900. Website: *www. asis.org*

Information Technology Association of America: 1616 N. Ft. Myer Drive, Suite 1300, Arlington, VA 22209-3106, Tel. 703/522-5055. Website: *www.itaa.org*

Society for Information Management: 401 North Michigan Ave., Chicago, IL 60611-4267, Tel. 312/644-6610. Website: *www.simnet.org*

Insurance

American Insurance Association: 1130 Connecticut Ave., NW, Suite 1000, Washington, DC 20036, Tel. 202/828-7100. Website: *www. aiadc.org*

Appraisers Association of America: 386 Park Avenue S., Suite 2000, New York, NY 10016, Tel. 212/899-5404. Website: *www.appraisers assoc.org*

National Association of Professional Insurance Agents: 400 N. Washington Street, Alexandria, VA 22314-2312, Tel. 703/836-9340. Website: *www.planet.com*

Management and Personnel

American Management Association International: 1601 Broadway, New York, NY 10019, Tel. 212/586-8100. Website: *www.amanet.org*

International Personnel Management Association: 1617 Duke St., Alexandria, VA 22314, Tel. 703/549-7100. Website: *www.ipma-hr.org*

Society For Human Resource Management: 1800 Duke Street, Alexandria, VA 22314, Tel. 703/548-3440. Website: *www.shrm.org*

Nursing

American Health Care Association: 1201 L Street, NW, Washington, DC 20005, Tel. 202/842-4444. Website: *www.ahca.org*

American Nurses' Association: 600 Maryland Avenue, SW, Suite 100, Washington, DC 20024, Tel. 202/651-7000. Website: *www.ana.org*

National Student Nurses Association: 555 W. 57th St., Suite 1327, New York, NY 10019, Tel. 212/571-2211. Website: *www.nsna.org*

Planning

American Planning Association: 122 S. Michigan Ave., Suite 1600, Chicago, IL 60603, Tel. 312/431-9100. Website: *www.planning.org*

Financial Planning Association: 3801 E. Florida Avenue, Suite 708, Denver, CO 80210-2571, Tel. 303/759-4900. Website: *www.fpanet.org*

Meeting Professionals International: 4455 LBJ Freeway, Suite 1200, Dallas, TX 75244-7718. Website: *www.mpiweb.org*

Psychology

American Psychiatric Association: 1400 K Street, NW, Washington, DC 20005, Tel. 202/682-6138. Website: *www.psych.org*

American Psychological Association: 750 First Street, NW, Washington, DC 20002-4242, Tel. 202/336-5500. Website: *www.apa.org*

National Mental Health Association: 1021 Prince St., Alexandria, VA 22314-2971, Tel. 703/684-7722. Website: *www.nmha.org*

Several other associations are organized around various population groups, such as women and minorities, that have professional interests. These organizations may cross-cut occupational fields, or they may group women and minorities within a particular profession or industry. Examples of such organizations for both women and minorities include the following:

American Association of University Women: 1111 16th Street, NW, Washington, DC 20036, Tel. 202/785-7700. Website: *www.aauw.org*

American Business Women's Association: 9100 Ward Parkway, Kansas City, MO 64114, Tel. 816/361-6621. Website: *www.abwahq.org*

LatinoLink: 601 Van Ness Avenue, #E-3309, San Francisco, CA 94102, Tel. 415/357-1172. Website: *www.latinolink.com*

National Association of Black Accountants: 7459-A Hanover Pkwy., Greenbelt, MD 20770, Tel. 301-4746222. Website: *www.afrika.com/nanbpwe*

Women Work! 1625 K Street, NW Suite 300, Washington, DC 20006, 202/467-6346. Website: *www.womenwork.org*

Job Search Networks

Several organizations function as networking groups for individuals seeking employment. Ostensibly known as job clubs and networking groups, most are organized to provide job search assistance for a particular population group, such as women, minorities, military personnel, alumni, mid-career individuals, or retirees. If, for example, you are over 40 years old and unemployed, you should consider joining a Forty Plus Club nearest you. The Forty Plus Clubs are self-help support groups that operate like job clubs. Members pay a monthly fee to join and participate in the day-to-day operation of the organization. They use club facilities to conduct job research, telephone prospective employers, attend job search meetings, and provide mutual support to other club members. At present 21 Forty Plus Clubs operate in ten states and the District of Columbia: ***www.fortyplus.com***. The Five O'Clock Club also provides similar career counseling and job search services to its members: ***www.fiveoclockclub.com***. Executive-level job seekers—those earning over $100,000 a year—often participate in ExecuNet: ***www.execunet.com***. Transitioning military personnel find these two professional associations useful for networking and employment assistance: The Retired Officers Association (***www.troa.org***) and the Non Commissioned Officers Association (***www.ncoausa.org***). They operate placement services and conduct job fairs.

8

Networking On the Internet

WITHIN THE PAST FEW YEARS, MUCH OF THE traditional job search has moved onto the Internet. Today, more and more employers and candidates first encounter each other through commercial online employment sites or the web pages of companies. Job seekers are well advised to spend as much as 30 percent of their job search time on the Internet where they can acquire information about both the job search and employers, enter their resume into online resume databases, and survey job postings. But the real advantage of using the Internet in your job search is the numerous networking opportunities available on the Internet in the form of chat groups, message boards, and forums.

The Basics

If you are not an Internet user, or your Internet skills need to be upgraded, you may want to acquire a copy of Angus J. Kennedy's excellent Internet book written in plain and engaging English: *The Rough Guide to the Internet* (New York: The Rough Guides). The publisher also offers a free electronic version on its website:

www.roughguides.com/internet/directory/index.html#tools

If you're not too familiar with how to conduct an online job search, which includes networking through chat groups, bulletin boards, and forums, you can quickly get up and running by consulting these excellent Internet employment resources:

CareerXroads 2001, Gerry Crispin and Mark Mehler
Job Searching Online For Dummies, Pam Dixon
The Guide to Internet Job Searching, Margaret Riley Dikel
    and Frances Roehm
100 Top Internet Job Sites, Kristina M. Ackley
Cyberspace Job Search Kit, Fred E. Jandt and Mary B. Nemich
e-Job Hunting, Eric Schlesinger and Susan Musich

Most of these books are available in bookstores or they can be ordered directly through Impact Publications (see order form on pages 132-133).

Online Networking

The Internet is an ever-changing medium for job seekers and employers. Today you will find thousands of Internet sites providing some type of employment service, be it advice on one or two aspects of your job search (assessment, resumes, interviews) or a fully integrated employment site offering job listings, a resume database, job search experts, online testing, chats, and forums. Sites such as Monster.com and CareerBuilder.com are known for both their functionality and longevity. Many other sites come and go. Indeed, perhaps as many at 30 percent of all Internet employment sites today will be out of business or merge with other sites within the next 18 months. But for now, the major Internet employment sites include these:

Monster.com:	*www.monster.com*
CareerBuilder:	*www.careerbuilder.com*
NationJob:	*www.nationjob.com*
FlipDog:	*www.flipdog.com*
Hot Jobs:	*www.hotjobs.com*
Vault.com:	*www.vault.com*
Headhunter.net:	*www.headhunter.net*
Career Journal:	*www.careerjournal.com*
Employment911.com:	*www.employment911.com*
WebFeet.com:	*www.webfeet.com*

PlanetRecruit:	*www.planetrecruit.com*
4Work:	*www.4work.com*
BestJobsUSA:	*www.bestjobsusa.com*
BrilliantPeople.com:	*www.brilliantpeople.com*
Career City:	*www.careercity.com*
JobOptions:	*www.joboptions.com*
JobTrak:	*www.jobtrak.com*
CampusCareerCenter:	*www.campuscareercenter.com*

These sites are rich in employment information and services; many include networking sections. For example, if you visit Monster.com's forum section, you'll discover numerous lively discussion groups organized around major occupational interests and groups, from international job seekers to transitioning military personnel:

http://community.monster.com/board

Newsgroups and Mailing Lists

Two major sources for online networking are Usenet newsgroups and mailing lists. Indeed, nearly 40,000 newsgroups currently function on the Internet. For information on available newsgroups and how to use them, visit these useful sites:

DejaNews:	*www.dejanews.com*
Liszt:	*www.liszt.com/news*
Usenet Info Center:	*http://metalab.unc.edu/usenet-i/*
	home.html
Questions:	*www.xs4all.nl/~wijnands/nnq/*
	grouplists.html

For information on over 100,000 mailing lists operating on the Internet, be sure to visit these key sites:

Liszt:	*www.liszt.com*
Paml.net:	*http://paml.net*
eGroups:	*www.egroups.com*
Topica:	*www.topica.com*
Listbot:	*www.listbot.com*

Index

A

Abuses, 3, 11-12
Answering machines, 88-90
Approach letters, 90-96
Associations, 118-125

B

Behavior:
   changing, 2, 15
   childhood, 9

C

Career:
   changes, 35-36, 59
   defined, 35
   development, 36-39
Closings:
   letter, 95
   telephone, 87-88
Cold calls, 79-81, 84-86
Communication, 1, 3, 8-9, 52-53
Communities, 24
Competition, 57-58
Connections, 10, 59
Contact list, 62-64
Contacts, 55, 67-69
Cooperation, 56

D

DC Web Women, 114
Demand, 111-112

E

Effectiveness, 71
Electronic networking, 28
Email, 52
Employers, 8, 12, 14, 15, 49, 52, 74-75
Employment firms, 59
Enclosures, 96
Ethics, 12, 14
ExecuNet, 125

F

Feedback, 108-110
Follow-up:
   actions, 108-110
   calls, 83
   resume, 83-84
   thank-you, 83
Five O'Clock Club, 114, 125
Forty Plus Club, 114, 125

G

Gatekeepers, 81

H

Hiring, 58
Honesty, 72-73

I

Informational interviews, 54, 73-78
Internet, 32-33, 126-128
Interviews:
   behavior-based, 14
   informational, 54, 73-107
   traditional, 14

J

Job:
   leads, 69-71
   referrals, 34
Job market:
   advertised, 32-35
   chaotic, 60
   hidden, 25, 32-35, 46
   images, 44-45
Job search:
   aggressive, 11
   effectiveness, 9
   long-distance, 24, 31
   network, 67-69
   organization, 40-43
   process, 36-40
   purpose of, 8

129

targeted, 58
time, 40-43
Jobs:
  asking for, 76
  finding, 46-47

L
Language, 3
Letters, 90-96
Linkages, 110-111
Luck, 57

M
Mailing lists, 128
Military, 125
Motivation, 15
Myths, 44-57

N
NCOA, 125
Networkers:
  abusive, 3, 10-11
  savvy, 2
Networking:
  abuses, 3, 10-11, 49-50
  activities, 3
  approach to, 12-13
  communities, 114-116
  defined, 3, 10-11
  electronic, 51-52
  examples, 29-31
  I.Q., 4-7
  lessons, 43
  long-distance, 24, 31, 56
  on-the-job, 110
  online, 126-128
  organizations, 113-125
  practical, 13
  process of, 28-29, 48
  purpose of, 28-29
  realities, 45-59
  results, 4
  savvy, 2
  skills, 3, 18
  techniques, 28-29, 48-49
  telephone, 78-90
Networks:
  building, 61-73
  community level, 24-27
  defining, 19
  electronic, 28
  expanding, 64-65
  identifying, 61-62
  individual level, 20-22

organizational level, 22-24
  types of, 19
Newsgroups, 128

O
Online networking, 125-128
Openers, 95
Opportunity structures, 25, 27
Organizations, 113-125
Orlando, 31

P
Persistence, 67
Personnel offices, 59, 77
Planning, 40, 57
Politics, 58
Probability, 65, 70
Professional associations, 24, 50-51,
  113-114
Prospecting, 65-67
Purpose, 9

Q
Qualifications, 8-9
Questions, 97-104

R
Referrals, 55-56, 81-82, 109
Rejections, 57, 66, 71-72, 75-76
Remembered, 101, 109
Research, 117
Resumes, 53-54
Role playing, 12-14

S
Serendipity, 1-6
Skills, 14
Sincerity, 72-73
Strangers, 1-2, 8-9, 56-57
Success, 8, 10, 106-107

T
Telephone, 65, 69-71, 78-90
Thank-you letters, 104-105
TROA, 125

V
Vacancy announcements, 86-87
Voice mail, 88-90

W
Washington, DC, 25-27, 114-116
Websites, 126-128

The Authors

RON AND CARYL KRANNICH, PH.Ds, ARE TWO OF America's leading career and travel writers who have authored more than 50 books. A former Peace Corps Volunteer and Fulbright Scholar, Ron received his Ph.D. in Political Science from Northern Illinois University. Caryl received her Ph.D. in Speech Communication from Penn State University. They operate Development Concepts Incorporated, a training, consulting, and publishing firm.

Ron and Caryl are both former university professors, high school teachers, management trainers, and consultants. As trainers and consultants, they have completed numerous projects on management, career development, local government, population planning, and rural development in the United States and abroad.

The Krannichs' career books focus on key job search skills, military and civilian career transitions, government and international careers, travel jobs, and nonprofit organizations. Their body of work represents one of today's most comprehensive collections of career writing. Their books are widely available in bookstores, libraries, and career centers.

Authors of 19 travel-shopping guidebooks on various destinations around the world, Ron and Caryl continue to pursue their international and travel interests through their innovative *Treasures and Pleasures of . . . Best of the Best* travel-shopping series and related website: *www.ishoparoundtheworld.com*. When not found at their home and business in Virginia, they are probably somewhere in Europe, Asia, Africa, the Middle East, the South Pacific, or the Caribbean and South America pursuing their other passion—researching and writing about quality arts and antiques.

As both career and travel experts, the Krannichs' work is frequently featured in major newspapers, magazines, and newsletters as well as on radio, television, and the Internet. They can be contacted through the publisher: *krannich@impactpublications.com*.

Career Resources

THE FOLLOWING CAREER RESOURCES, MANY OF WHICH were mentioned in previous chapters, are available directly from Impact Publications. Complete the following form or list the titles, include postage (see formula at the end), enclose payment, and send your order to:

IMPACT PUBLICATIONS
9104 Manassas Drive, Suite N
Manassas Park, VA 20111-5211
1-800-361-1055 (orders only)
Tel. 703/361-7300 or Fax 703/335-9486
Email address: *orders@impactpublications.com*
Quick & easy online ordering: *www.impactpublications.com*

Orders from individuals must be prepaid by check, moneyorder, Visa, MasterCard, or American Express. We accept telephone and fax orders.

Qty.	TITLES	Price	TOTAL

Networking

Qty.	TITLES	Price	TOTAL
___	Dig Your Well Before You're Thirsty	$14.95	___
___	A Foot in the Door	14.95	___
___	Golden Rule of Schmoozing	12.95	.
___	Great Connections	11.95	___
___	How to Work a Room	14.00	___
___	Masters of Networking	16.95	___
___	Networking For Everyone	16.95	___
___	Networking Smart	22.95	___
___	Power Networking	14.95	___
___	People Power	14.95	___
___	Power Networking	12.95	___
___	Power Schmoozing	14.95	___
___	The Power to Get In	14.95	___
___	**The Savvy Networker**	13.95	___
___	Secrets of Savvy Networking	13.99	___

Key Directories

Qty.	TITLES	Price	TOTAL
___	Encyclopedia of Associations (National, 3 volumes)	$520.00	___
___	National Trade and Professional Associations	129.95	___

Internet Job Search and Online Networking

___	100 Top Internet Job Sites	$12.95	___
___	CareerXroads 2001	26.95	___
___	Cyberspace Job Search Kit	18.95	___
___	e-Job Hunting	17.99	___
___	Guide to Internet Job Searching	14.95	___
___	Job Searching Online For Dummies	24.99	___

Other Great Career Resources

___	100 Great Jobs and How to Get Them	$17.95	___
___	101 Dynamite Answers to Interview Questions	12.95	___
___	101 Dynamite Questions to Ask At Your Job Interview	14.95	___
___	Best Jobs For the 21st Century	19.95	___
___	Change Your Job, Change Your Life	17.95	___
___	Dynamite Cover Letters	14.95	___
___	Dynamite Resumes	14.95	___
___	Dynamite Salary Negotiations	15.95	___
___	Get a Raise in 7 Days	14.95	___
___	High Impact Resumes & Letters	19.95	___
___	Interview For Success	15.95	___
___	Proof of Performance	17.95	___
___	The Savvy Interviewer	10.95	___
___	What Color Is Your Parachute?	16.95	___

SUBTOTAL   ___

Virginia residents add 4½% sales tax   ___

POSTAGE/HANDLING ($5 for first
product and 8% of SUBTOTAL over $30) $5.00

8% of SUBTOTAL over $30 --------------------------   ___

TOTAL ENCLOSED ----------------------   ___

NAME _____

ADDRESS _____

_____

_____

❑ I enclose check/moneyorder for $ _____ made payable to
IMPACT PUBLICATIONS.

❑ Please charge $ _____ to my credit card:
❑ Visa   ❑ MasterCard   ❑ American Express   ❑ Discover

Card # _____

Expiration date: _____/_____

Signature _____

The Click and Easy™ Online Resource Centers

Books, videos, software, training materials, articles, and advice for job seekers, employers, HR professionals, schools, and libraries

Visit us online for all your career and travel needs:

www.impactpublications.com
(career superstore and Impact Publications)

––––––––––

www.winningthejob.com
(career articles and advice)

––––––––––

www.contentforcareers.com
(syndicated career content for job seekers, employees, and Intranets)

––––––––––

www.greentogray.com
www.bluetogray.com
(military transition databases and content)

––––––––––

www.ishoparoundtheworld.com
(unique international travel-shopping center)